SpringerBriefs in Education

We are delighted to announce SpringerBriefs in Education, an innovative product type that combines elements of both journals and books. Briefs present concise summaries of cutting-edge research and practical applications in education. Featuring compact volumes of 50 to 125 pages, the SpringerBriefs in Education allow authors to present their ideas and readers to absorb them with a minimal time investment. Briefs are published as part of Springer's eBook Collection. In addition, Briefs are available for individual print and electronic purchase.

SpringerBriefs in Education cover a broad range of educational fields such as: Science Education, Higher Education, Educational Psychology, Assessment & Evaluation, Language Education, Mathematics Education, Educational Technology, Medical Education and Educational Policy.

SpringerBriefs typically offer an outlet for:

- An introduction to a (sub)field in education summarizing and giving an overview of theories, issues, core concepts and/or key literature in a particular field
- A timely report of state-of-the art analytical techniques and instruments in the field of educational research
- A presentation of core educational concepts
- An overview of a testing and evaluation method
- A snapshot of a hot or emerging topic or policy change
- An in-depth case study
- A literature review
- A report/review study of a survey
- An elaborated thesis

Both solicited and unsolicited manuscripts are considered for publication in the SpringerBriefs in Education series. Potential authors are warmly invited to complete and submit the Briefs Author Proposal form. All projects will be submitted to editorial review by editorial advisors.

SpringerBriefs are characterized by expedited production schedules with the aim for publication 8 to 12 weeks after acceptance and fast, global electronic dissemination through our online platform SpringerLink. The standard concise author contracts guarantee that:

- an individual ISBN is assigned to each manuscript
- each manuscript is copyrighted in the name of the author
- the author retains the right to post the pre-publication version on his/her website or that of his/her institution

More information about this series at http://www.springer.com/series/8914

Fernando M. Reimers

Educating Students to Improve the World

Fernando M. Reimers
Harvard Graduate School of Education
Cambridge, MA, USA

ISSN 2211-1921 ISSN 2211-193X (electronic)
SpringerBriefs in Education
ISBN 978-981-15-3886-5 ISBN 978-981-15-3887-2 (eBook)
https://doi.org/10.1007/978-981-15-3887-2

© The Editor(s) (if applicable) and The Author(s) 2020. This book is an open access publication.
Open Access This book is licensed under the terms of the Creative Commons Attribution 4.0 International License (http://creativecommons.org/licenses/by/4.0/), which permits use, sharing, adaptation, distribution and reproduction in any medium or format, as long as you give appropriate credit to the original author(s) and the source, provide a link to the Creative Commons license and indicate if changes were made.
The images or other third party material in this book are included in the book's Creative Commons license, unless indicated otherwise in a credit line to the material. If material is not included in the book's Creative Commons license and your intended use is not permitted by statutory regulation or exceeds the permitted use, you will need to obtain permission directly from the copyright holder.
The use of general descriptive names, registered names, trademarks, service marks, etc. in this publication does not imply, even in the absence of a specific statement, that such names are exempt from the relevant protective laws and regulations and therefore free for general use.
The publisher, the authors and the editors are safe to assume that the advice and information in this book are believed to be true and accurate at the date of publication. Neither the publisher nor the authors or the editors give a warranty, expressed or implied, with respect to the material contained herein or for any errors or omissions that may have been made. The publisher remains neutral with regard to jurisdictional claims in published maps and institutional affiliations.

This Springer imprint is published by the registered company Springer Nature Singapore Pte Ltd.
The registered company address is: 152 Beach Road, #21-01/04 Gateway East, Singapore 189721, Singapore

Preface

The shared nature of many of the current concerns and opportunities of humanity, from climate change to trade, pandemics to security, and governance to advancing science, require that people across the world are educated to understand them, care about them, and have the skills to address them collaboratively, from their respective spheres of influence. Global education is the domain of scholarship and of practice which focuses on developing such competencies. This field has a long history, albeit one that comprises more small-scale successes than accounts of large-scale educational transformations of educational institutions that succeed at educating global citizens. A review of the theoretical scholarship, and of the literature on practice, suggests that there have not been sufficiently productive interactions between those two domains.

At times when the nature of our global challenges underscores the urgency of more effective skills for global understanding and collaboration, this book is an attempt to bring closer together the worlds of scholarship and practice in global education, proposing a conceptual approach to advancing it that addresses five core dimensions of the process: cultural, psychological, professional, institutional, and political. Relying on this theory, I then discuss an extensive body of research and practice-oriented literature on global education, drawing out the implications to lead global education programs.

My own involvement with the field of global education began serendipitously. My early career involved me in carrying out research and policy analysis to advise governments around the world on education policy. This interest in policy reform then took me to the World Bank where I worked in the design of large-scale programs of educational improvement.

From this work on policy reform, I transitioned to teaching graduate students at the Harvard Graduate School of Education in the areas of education policy and international development. As schools of education, in the United States at least, are somewhat provincial in their foci, more adept at studying matters of domestic import than at engaging in comparative analysis to advance the field of education, I soon found myself making the case for a comparative perspective, first to my students and colleagues, and subsequently to other education leaders. As I advocated for greater reliance on comparative approaches in education, my scholarly interests evolved from the study of the educational conditions which supported access and learning for low income and otherwise marginalized students in the developing world to the field of civic education. I began to see civic competencies as essential to the empowerment of students to become architects of their own lives, and civic education as the logical pathway to that empowerment.

The convergence of both interests, civics and comparative education, led me to think of global education as a 'new civics' of the twenty-first century, an indispensable dimension of civic education and empowerment in a world ever more integrated and interdependent. What began as work on a conceptual level, writing some chapters and journal articles conceptualizing and making the case for this new civics, eventually took me to developing curriculum materials to support teachers interested in advancing intentional efforts to educating students to be globally aware and to organizing programs of professional development to support them in that undertaking. In this way, I came to see global education as a way to bring challenges of the real world to the school, in the form of challenging, rigorous and high-quality curriculum which would help students develop the capacity to understand and participate in a world ever more globally interdependent, and in the form of the essential professional development teachers would need if they were going to deliver on that aspiration.

I created an approach of curriculum development which aligned instruction with capacious visions of an inclusive world, as articulated in the United Nations Sustainable Development Goals and in the United Nations Universal Declaration of Human Rights. The interest that some of those materials generated among teachers and others deepened my involvement with efforts of educators advancing a practice of global education. These efforts in global education became integrated into other research I was working on to understand how to transform public education systems, the focus of the Global Education Innovation Initiative, a cross-national effort I lead at Harvard University.

This book is the result of the fusion of both such interests in global education and in the comparative study of large-scale change to make education relevant. For one of the studies carried out as part of the Global Education Innovation Initiative, a large comparative study of education reform examining how various nations had transformed the goals of education, I developed a conceptual framework to explain how those various reforms had been approached. I wrote that theoretical framework, which served as the introductory chapter of another book, as I was concluding three years of work synthesizing research on global education and theorizing the work I had engaged in for over a decade supporting global educators through curriculum materials and professional development. Inevitably, these two efforts reinforced one another, and the framework I sketched to account for the comparative analysis of reforms quickly shaped the intellectual architecture of this book on global education.

Many people have educated me on the topics I discuss in this book and, in ways big and small, influenced the development of the ideas I present in this book. First and foremost my graduate students at Harvard, who as my most reliable interlocutors have provided continuous and significant intellectual stimulus for the ideas developed in this book. Then, my colleagues who advance efforts of global education practice in schools around the world and who, in inviting me to share ideas with them, have taught me more than I have taught them. They include Luis Enrique Garcia de Brigard, founder of Envoys, Chris Whittle, Tyler Tingley, and their colleagues as they founded the Avenues School and invited me to design the World Course, Nieves Segovia, and her colleagues at the SEK Schools, Kate Berseth, vice-president of EF, Anthony Jackson at the Asia Society, Gabriela Ramos and Andreas Schleicher at the OECD, Vikas Pota at the Varkey Education Foundation, Giovanna Barzano and Rete Dialogues, Marjorie Tiven at the Global Cities Program at Bloomberg Philanthropies, Ross Weissman at Knovva, Joseph Carvin at One World, Jennifer Manise at the Longview Foundation, Veronica Boix-Mansilla at Project Zero, Robert Adams at the National Education Education Foundation, Jennifer Boyle, and her colleagues at Primary Source. To them and all others who trusted me to engage with their efforts, my deepest gratitude for what I learned from them and from our collaborations.

Many of the education organizations on whose boards I have served advanced global education in several ways, and I have learned from that work, from their staff, and from my fellow board members. My long-standing collaborations with colleagues in UNESCO, from the time when the organization published my first book, three decades ago, to my participation on some of the consultations for the preparation of the Delors Report, to my most recent engagement as member of the commission on the Futures of Education, have been a source of intellectual stimulation and inspiration to advance my understanding of the topics discussed in this book. I am grateful to Stefania Giannini, Director of Education at UNESCO and to Irina Bokova, former Director General at UNESCO, and to their colleagues for our collaborations to advance global education. In WorldTeach, my colleagues on the board, our CEO Mitra Shavarini and our staff, taught me much about high-quality global education programming, and about the challenges of sustaining such programs. I have learned a great deal about civic education from Roger Brooks, President of Facing History and Ourselves, and from my colleagues on the board and from the excellent staff in the organization. Teach for All, an organization depending on a remarkable network of global citizens advancing educational opportunity in more than fifty countries is an ongoing source of learning for me, from collaborations with the CEO and founder Wendy Kopp, with my fellow members on the board and from our staff.

At Harvard, serving on the University Committee of International Projects for over a decade, and on the faculty boards of the Centers for African Studies, Asian Studies, Latin American Studies, and China Fund has educated me on the many ways in which a research university can educate global citizens. My graduate students are a continuous source of inspiration and learning with their cosmopolitanism and global citizenship. Between 2010 and 2016, collaborations with seventy-five of my graduate students on the development of three curriculum resources aligned with the UN Sustainable Development Goals helped translate many of my ideas on global education into usable resources which could be tested in practice. In addition, the translation of these books into multiple languages, and their use by thousands of educators across the world, provided me a very rich laboratory of practice from which many of the ideas presented in this book stemmed.

I have learned much from the thousands of global educators who participated in an annual think tank on global education I led at Harvard over the last decade, and from my colleague Mitalene Fletcher, who co-led the think tank with me. Other colleagues at the Harvard Graduate School of Education have provided, over many years, an energizing intellectual community, and I have benefited from conversations with Howard Gardner, Jal Mehta, Felipe Barrera-Osorio, Sarah Dryden-Peterson, Paola Uccelli, Richard Light, Paul Harris, Patricia Graham, Jerome Murphy, Paul Reville, Chris Dede, Jim Honan, Meira Levinson, Julie Reuben, Monica Higgins, Matt Miller, Mary Grassa O'Neill, Karen Mapp, Richard Elmore, Catherine Snow, Pamela Mason, Nonie Lesaux, Richard Murnane, and others. My current and past Teaching Fellows and Research Assistants have taught me a great deal about global education, I am especially indebted to Nell O'Donnell-Weber, Ana Teresa Toro, Paul Moch Islas, Uche Amaeche, Tatiana Shevchenko, Vanessa Beary, Isabelle Byusa and Vidur Chopra. I have benefited from the support of various deans of the Harvard Graduate School of Education including Jerome Murphy, Ellen Lagemann, Katherine McCartney, Jim Ryan and Bridget Terry-Long.

My colleagues in the Global Education Innovation Initiative have considerably helped me better understand the process of educational change, and our many conversations and collaborations over seven years, and discussions with our board members and with the many colleagues who invited us to share our research, provided a nourishing intellectual context for the development of the ideas presented in this book.

Andy Hall, the coordinator of the International Education Policy Program I have directed at Harvard for the last two decades, my assistant Lee Marmor and my former assistant Kristin Foster have been essential collaborators in my practice as an educator of global citizens, on which much of the thinking in this book is based. Working with these three global citizens who do so much themselves to help educate others as global citizens is a source of daily inspiration.

I am also grateful to Nick Melchior and Lay Peng Ang, and to their colleagues at Springer, for their support and good care of this publication.

As with all of my projects, big and small, my biggest debt is to my wife and colleague, Professor Eleonora Villegas-Reimers, for everything I have learned with her and with her help, since we met at Harvard as graduate students in 1983. My hope is that the approach to global education I present here will be valuable not just to scholars in the field of global education, and of educational change, but that it will provide theoretical grounding to practitioners in the field of global education and allow more fruitful dialogue between the communities of academics and practitioners. I look forward to continuing to learn from those who try out the ideas offered here, make them their own, and transform them through their practice.

Cambridge, USA   Fernando M. Reimers

Contents

1	**Five Eyes to Educate Global Citizens. The Need for a Useful Theory of Global Education**	**1**
	1.1 A Cultural Perspective on Educational Change	10
	1.2 A Psychological Perspective on Educational Change	12
	1.3 A Professional Perspective on Educational Change	16
	1.4 An Institutional Perspective on Educational Change	18
	1.5 A Political Perspective on Educational Change	21
	References	22
2	**What Is Global Education and Why Does It Matter?**	**25**
	References	28
3	**A Cultural Perspective and Global Education**	**31**
	3.1 The Long Roots of Global Education	31
	3.2 Growing Interest in Global Education	36
	3.3 Recent Imperatives for Global Education	39
	References	50
4	**A Psychological Perspective and Global Education**	**53**
	References	63
5	**A Professional Perspective and Global Education**	**65**
	5.1 Helping Teachers Gain Knowledge and Skills in Global Education	66
	5.2 Engaging Teachers as Creators of Expert Knowledge in Global Education	70
	References	74
6	**An Institutional Perspective and Global Education**	**77**
	6.1 Standards	78
	6.2 Curriculum and Pedagogy	80
	6.3 Instructional Resources	104

  6.4 Assessment 105
  6.5 Staff and Development 107
  6.6 School Organization 113
  References 116

7 A Political Perspective and Global Education 121
  References 126

8 Conclusions. Integrating the Five Perspectives 129

Chapter 1
Five Eyes to Educate Global Citizens. The Need for a Useful Theory of Global Education

This book examines how to educate students to be globally aware, globally minded, and globally proficient. It explains why educating students as global citizens matters for students, for schools, and for the future of humanity. While a growing number of parents and educators understand the importance of these goals, significantly less of them act on that awareness effectively. This gap between awareness and action is rooted in a wide schism between scholarship on global education and practice. As a result of this gap, two disconnected strands of literature guide, or more appropriately provide insufficient guidance, to the field: academic literature and practical guides.

Much of what has been written on global education is long on explaining why it should be done, and what global education means and short on providing details on how to implement effective instruction. No doubt one reason academic conversations about global education can be protracted, is because there is contention regarding the rationale and definition of the core constructs of the field of global education. Some see it as a way to help people adapt to increasing globalization, while others as a way to help them challenge that process. Still others view it as a way to serve the needs of businesses as they integrate globally, and others as a way to educate students to advance social inclusion and human rights (Davies et al. 2018). As a result of this contention on what goals should be advanced by global citizenship education, the rich academic conversation about purposes is more limited when it comes to the details on the pragmatics of making these purposes happen in schools. This academic conversation about global education has been woefully disconnected from practice, with the voices of teachers and school leaders largely missing and with a very thin empirical base examining what works, for whom, in what context or with what short or long-term consequences. As a result, there is no theory or theories of global education which has visible connection to the practice of the enterprise.

Dissociated from these academic debates, a separate set of conversations more connected to the practice of global education happens in publications of various sorts and in guides to support the introduction of global education in schools, these do offer practical guidance to actually develop a global education program (Klein 2016; Longview Foundation 2008; OECD and Asia Society 2018; Tavangar and Mladic-Morales 2014; UNESCO 2015, 2017). In contrast to the academic scholarship which has limited grounding in practice, these practical tools are almost exclusively about practice, with limited theoretical and conceptual grounding. These under-theorized and under-researched guides offer approaches which address partial elements of what it takes to transform the institutions of education, but lack the comprehensiveness and system perspective necessary to transform the culture of teaching and learning and are devoid of solid empirical evidence. The lack of an explicit theoretical foundation undergirding these guides of suggestions leaves those teachers and education leaders who want to use those generic tools and lists of activities with limited conceptual support to make sound professional judgments about how to develop a program of global education which is responsive to the particular needs and context of their students, their school and their community. Furthermore, the absence of a theoretical framework in support of these practical resources limits the ability to draw lessons from the application of these frameworks which can advance a theoretical foundation for this work.

As a result of this schism, the field of global education is missing a good theory, in the sense in which Kurt Lewin used the term in 1952 when he wrote "There is nothing more practical than a good theory," (Lewin 1952, p. 169).

> Lewin's message was twofold: theorists should try to provide new ideas for understanding or conceptualizing a (problematic) situation, ideas which may suggest potentially fruitful new avenues of dealing with that situation. Conversely, applied researchers should provide theorists with key information and facts relevant to solving a practical problem, facts that need to be conceptualized in a detailed and coherent manner. More generally, theorists should strive to create theories that can be used to solve social or practical problems, and practitioners and researchers in applied psychology should make use of available scientific theory. (Vansteenkiste and Sheldon 2006, p. 63)

The purpose of this book is to bring together these two worlds of scholarship and practice, offering a theoretical multidimensional model of global education that places teachers, school principals, and other school-level actors at the center of defining what global education should be and how it should be done and which can support their professional choices with a systemic and comprehensive approach to developing programs of global education that are responsive to the needs and characteristics of specific schools and local contexts. To explicate this theoretical framework I draw on and synthesize a vast body of empirical scholarship and evidence, as well as on an analysis of the historical roots of the field. The book offers an intellectual approach to global education, as an attempt to professionalize a field more intentionally connecting scholarship and practice.

There are at least two reasons why teachers and education leaders may want to make global education a priority of the institutions they lead. The first is that doing so would help make what happens in school more relevant to the world in which students are growing up. The second is that in focusing on the adaptive challenge of making education relevant, educators will engage in practices of transformation that will also make learning and teaching more effective and engaging, for students as well as for teachers. Leading change to make education relevant is about leading educational change for a meaningful purpose. In other words, taking on the challenge of aligning instruction with a global set of goals can help revisit how we think of teaching and learning with benefits for the entirety of the educational enterprise. Global education should not be seen as an add-on, as an additional mandate or aspiration that needs to be inserted into an already existing crowded curriculum, or that needs to be introduced in its own silo in the school. Instead, global education can be an integrative force of the entire curriculum, that can help bring together what is more often than not a fragmented curriculum, provide coherence and make visible for students how what they learn in school actually matters to their future. To lead this process of educational change effectively, though, educators will need to think systemically and multidimensionally about the process. As they do so, they will engage in systemic transformation that actually influences instruction, a goal which has eluded many reform efforts in the past.

Arguably, helping every student develop a sense of purpose, intellectual autonomy, and emotional maturity to have ideas about what efforts are worth pursuing, is one of the most important goals of education. Engaging students with real world challenges is a way to help them develop that sense of purpose. The results of a recent survey of 15-year olds conducted by the OECD reveal that many of them lack such sense of purpose, as seen in Table 1.1. On average, among OECD countries, one in three 15-year olds enrolled in school do not think their life has clear meaning or purpose, have not discovered a satisfactory meaning in life or have a clear sense of what gives meaning to their lives. Whereas in some countries four out of every five students see purpose to their lives (such as is the case in Panama, Albania, Indonesia, Macedonia, the Dominican Republic, Peru, Mexico, Colombia, Costa Rica, and other countries) there are other countries where only three in five students see purpose to their lives, such as in Japan, Taipei, the United Kingdom, Macao, the Czech Republic, Ireland, the Netherlands, Sweden, Australia, and others. Helping students develop a sense of themselves in the world would help them develop purpose.

While the desire to educate global citizens is not new, as will be discussed in greater detail later in this book, most schools around the world are not adequately educating students to be global citizens.

The United Nations and UNESCO, among others, have over many decades advocated for the importance of global education. Following its first report on the Future of Education, in 1974 UNESCO presented to all member states, the International Recommendation concerning Education for International Understanding, Co-operation and Peace and Education relating to Human Rights and Fundamental Freedoms, which was adopted at the 18th General Conference of Ministers of Education (UNESCO 1974).

Additional impetus for the idea of global citizenship education was provided by the compact of development adopted at the annual general conference of the United Nations, in September of 2015, at which the governments of the nations participating embraced the goal of sustainable development, identifying seventeen goals and a series of specific targets, and highlighting the pivotal role education should play in the achievement of all other goals. The fourth Sustainable Development Goal "Ensure inclusive and equitable quality education and promote lifelong learning opportunities for all," explicitly mentions global citizenship education as one of the goals of education for all in target 4.7:

Table 1.1 Students' sense of meaning in life

	Percentage of students who agreed or strongly agreed with the following statement		
	My life has clear meaning or purpose	I have discovered a satisfactory meaning in life	I have a clear sense of what gives meaning to my life
Panama	86	82	85
Albania	90	80	86
Indonesia	93	90	89
North Macedonia	85	81	86
Dominican Republic	85	79	82
Peru	87	83	84
Mexico	86	81	83
Colombia	88	80	83
Kosovo	89	80	87
Costa Rica	85	75	79
Baku (Azerbaijan)	84	76	82
Kazakhstan	88	77	84
Philippines	84	83	85
Jordan	82	73	82
Thailand	86	83	89
Morocco	84	74	82
Belarus	88	83	81
United Arab Emirates	80	74	78
Saudi Arabia	85	65	86
Vietnam	88	80	90
Montenegro	81	73	76
Moldova	85	74	81
Bosnia and Herzegovina	82	77	81
Qatar	76	72	77
Romania	79	74	74
Lebanon	72	68	77
Switzerland	73	71	71
Chile	75	67	70
Croatia	77	68	71
Serbia	76	68	73
Austria	69	65	70

(continued)

Table 1.1 (continued)

	Percentage of students who agreed or strongly agreed with the following statement		
	My life has clear meaning or purpose	I have discovered a satisfactory meaning in life	I have a clear sense of what gives meaning to my life
Turkey	81	64	66
United States	71	65	69
Lithuania	72	63	71
Russia	73	68	73
Germany	68	65	68
Malaysia	85	60	76
France	72	69	65
Spain	70	66	68
Georgia	78	61	75
Korea	67	65	68
Portugal	70	68	71
Luxembourg	69	66	67
B-S-J-Z (China)	77	57	71
Brazil	76	67	65
Brunei Darussalam	76	67	76
Uruguay	69	65	70
Argentina	71	58	72
Finland	66	70	71
Bulgaria	76	60	67
Greece	63	66	68
Slovenia	68	65	67
OECD average	68	62	66
Ukraine	76	53	68
Belgium (Flemish)	71	65	68
Denmark	62	63	68
Hong Kong (China)	69	64	67
Slovak Republic	66	59	66
Malta	66	63	67
Estonia	67	61	64
Poland	66	56	66
Latvia	64	61	65
Iceland	65	54	60

(continued)

Table 1.1 (continued)

	Percentage of students who agreed or strongly agreed with the following statement		
	My life has clear meaning or purpose	I have discovered a satisfactory meaning in life	I have a clear sense of what gives meaning to my life
Australia	62	59	64
Italy	67	56	62
Sweden	60	57	63
Hungary	74	50	48
Netherlands	63	53	64
Ireland	60	53	60
Czech Republic	59	52	57
Macao (China)	60	48	56
United Kingdom	57	52	58
Chinese Taipei	64	43	52
Japan	56	41	40

Source OECD (2019d, Table III.B1.11.14)

> By 2030, ensure that all learners acquire the knowledge and skills needed to promote sustainable development, including, among others, through education for sustainable development and sustainable lifestyles, human rights, gender equality, promotion of a culture of peace and non violence, global citizenship and appreciation of cultural diversity and of culture's contribution to sustainable development. (UN 2020)

Over time, the development and dissemination of these ideas have caused governments to revise and expand national standards and curriculum. UNESCO carries out periodic consultations to member states to assess the extent to which the goals of the 1974 recommendation are reflected in education policies and in the curriculum. The most recent consultation, to which 83 out of 195 member states responded, reports improvements in implementing the guiding principles of the 1974 recommendation. Among the respondents, 68% indicate that these principles are fully integrated into education policies, and an additional 51% indicate that they are somewhat reflected. All countries report that the curriculum includes goals reflecting peace and non-violence, 99% include human rights and fundamental freedoms, 96% include cultural diversity, and 99% include environmental sustainability goals (UNESCO 2018, Fig. 6). The same survey shows that there is a disconnect between the inclusion of these goals in the curriculum and the extent to which they are also incorporated in teacher education programs. Only 19% of the countries report that these goals are fully integrated in teacher preparation programs, and an additional 93% indicate that they are only somewhat integrated (UNESCO 2018, Fig. 13).

An in-depth analysis of policy documents in ten countries with an expressed commitment to Education for Sustainable Development and Global Citizenship Education undertaken by UNESCO, revealed that in all these countries there are abundant references to both of these concepts, and that they are expressed in terms of cognitive, socio-emotional, and behavioral dimensions (UNESCO 2019). In the documents examined in these countries—Costa Rica, Japan, Kenya, Lebanon, Mexico, Morocco, Portugal, Republic of Korea, Rwanda, and Sweden—there were almost twice as many references to Global Citizenship Education (representing about 60% of the references) than to Education for Sustainable Development (representing about 30%) across national laws, strategic plans and policies, national curriculum frameworks, programmatic documents, and subject-specific curriculum. These references were present across various subjects in the curriculum, and the emphasis on cognitive dimensions, relative to socio-emotional and behavioral, increased in secondary education (Ibid).

One reason many past attempts to include global education in the curriculum and to translate those broadened aspirations into actual instructional practice have failed is because they have been short on details that could guide implementation, as if simply by wishing that education were more global it would become so. Advocacy, even if successful in persuading teachers and principals that they should teach students about the world, is woefully insufficient to provide guidance on what to do differently in the classroom. Another reason previous attempts have failed is because they have been partial and fragmented, ignoring the system of interdependent components which sustain the culture of education. A global education curriculum is not self-executing; it is unlikely to change instruction if it is not accompanied by the necessary support for teachers to develop the necessary skills to teach it, or by the necessary support from school leaders and parents, or if it does not address how it will be integrated into the other demands for students and teachers use of instructional time. A systemic approach to global education has been lacking in much of what has been attempted to date. It is no wonder that such efforts have lacked stickiness to endure or the capacity to scale.

These challenges faced by efforts at making instruction more global are not unique to global education. Much of the pre-existing knowledge about the results of efforts to change the curriculum and to transform instruction, often based on the study of experiences in the United States, argues that educational institutions have changed very little, that they are refractory to attempts to change them, and that many reforms fail at transforming the basic grammar of schooling (Tyack and Tobin 1994; Tyack and Cuban 1995; Olson 2003). Richard Elmore's conclusion about why most education reforms in the United States have failed to influence instruction illustrates this perspective:

> a systemic incapacity of U.S. schools and the practitioners who work in them, to develop, incorporate and extend new ideas about teaching in anything but a small fraction of schools and classrooms. This incapacity, I argue, is rooted primarily in the incentive structures in which teachers and administrators work. (Elmore 1996, p. 1)

Such failure of many past attempts to transform instruction, including attempts to introduce global education in the curriculum, is the predictable outcome of relying on a limited set of mental models about how schools work and change. Using a multidimensional model to guide efforts to advance global education is likely to produce better results because education systems are multidimensional. Education institutions do not change because a teacher brings a new lesson, or a new set of lessons, or even a new curriculum. The way in which those changes ultimately transform the culture of education, what Elmore has called the *instructional core*, or what Tyack and Cuban have called the *grammar of schooling* is as a result of the interactions between those changes and the other conditions present in school, including other instructional demands and priorities, teacher capacity, parental and student expectations, and assessments. To produce change we need to consider these elements of the institutions of education. But effective change requires more than thinking systemically about schools as institutions. A comprehensive model must reflect the multidimensional nature of the education enterprise, addressing global education from a cultural, psychological, professional, institutional, and political perspective.

It is as a disciplinary and methodological requirement that the study of the process of educational change has focused on a limited set of constructs and explanations. But just because different scholars have approached the process of change as either a cultural, or psychological, or professional, or institutional or political object of study does not reduce such process to the elements addressed by each of these singular perspectives. The process of change is, simultaneously, one where these five perspectives operate together. When teachers and school leaders plan a program of global education, they do not address instruction and leadership through the singular aspects that each of these five perspectives highlight. Practitioners face the process of change full swoop, as a totality, they experience schools not as the fragments which scholarly analysis breaks them into in an attempt to explain them, but as a whole. As a result, in trying to build a useful theory of school change to make education relevant, it is essential that the theory helps to integrate these five perspectives, and in so doing captures the holistic nature of education and of the change process. I have elsewhere used this framework to explain national-level reforms that broadened the goals of the curriculum, in this chapter I draw on that work and expand on it (Reimers 2020).

Together, these five perspectives offer a comprehensive approach to integrating much of what is known about how students learn and how schools change. These perspectives are complementary; each of them focuses on certain elements of the change process. The cultural perspective, for example, is about the big picture of how schools relate to the larger society in terms of the broader set of societal hopes for schools, norms, and values which define what are accepted educational goals and practices and in terms of how those social expectations change. The psychological perspective illustrates the theories of learning which undergird the learning and teaching process. The professional perspective focuses on how expertise is inserted into professional roles to advance teaching and learning. The institutional perspective attends to the various structures, processes, and resources that provide resiliency to the system of education, governing the interactions among the actors that form the system and providing stability and meaning to teaching and learning. The political perspective illustrates how the interests of various groups are negotiated and conflicts among those interests resolved, resulting in a particular culture of education.

Each perspective[1] focuses on a series of constructs, logically related, which can help explain partial aspects of the process of change. Some of the elements of introducing global education in schools may more logically fit with a singular perspective, others may correspond to more than one perspective. For example, the transformation of work, as a result of the use of technology and artificial intelligence, creates new cognitive demands, and demands in information literacy and computational thinking, among participants in the labor market. This shift is in part a cultural shift, a result of changes in the external environment that modify what is expected of schools, but it is also a political shift, particularly if the new demands of employers or workers translate into organized efforts to influence the curriculum or of concerns over unemployment raise the interest of ordinary citizens in education.

These five perspectives are aligned with and build upon other conceptualizations of organizations and of schools. Organizational theorists Lee Bolman and Terry Deal, for example, argued that much of the scholarship on organizations can be usefully synthesized in four *frames*: structural, human resources, political, and symbolic (Bolman and Deal 1991). While there is no one-to-one correspondence between the four frames proposed by Bolman and Deal and the five perspectives to study the process of change I present here, the *structural frame* focuses on concepts which correspond to what I have termed an institutional perspective, *human resources* to a professional perspective, *political* to the perspective of the same name, and *symbolic* to a cultural perspective.

School effectiveness scholar Jaap Scheerens summarizes the theoretical views on organizational effectiveness in his conceptualization of school effectiveness as: *economic rationality*, *organic systems model*, *human relations approach*, *bureaucracy* and *political* (Scheerens 2000, p. 23–26). There is also some correspondence between the organic systems model, which emphasizes adaptation of school systems to their external environment, and what I call a cultural perspective; between the bureaucratic perspective and what I call an institutional perspective, and between the political perspective which I call also political. Scheeren's emphasis for each of these models differs from mine and his conceptualization lacks a psychological and a professional perspective.

Professor David Olson has also contrasted the *institutional* and *psychological* perspectives to study education reform arguing that it is the lack of attention to the institutional dimensions of schooling that explains the failure of many efforts to incorporate ideas from psychology into schooling (Olson 2003). While I share Professor Olson's view that reform is at the same time an institutional and a psychological process, I think it is essential to integrate additional perspectives to understand educational change: cultural, professional, and political.

---

[1] The presentation of these five perspectives in the remaining of this chapter draws extensively on my chapter in the book Audacious Education Purposes 2020.

1.1 A Cultural Perspective on Educational Change

A cultural perspective helps to see the "big picture" of how schools relate to the larger society. It emphasizes that educational practice is the result of shared expectations, norms, artifacts, and practices which define how education is broadly understood in a society. Such "culture of education" includes several interrelated domains: how educational institutions are understood to relate to other social institutions and to social purposes and values, how society sees teachers and learners, and how instruction is understood to take place.

Schools share their role in socializing the young with other institutions such as families, religious institutions, and civic organizations. Every society has expectations about what role schools should play, as well as about the appropriate activities to be carried out in the instructional sphere and what actions are "off limits." The key questions from this perspective are: what is the appropriate division of labor among schools and other socialization institutions in advancing social purposes and values? Are schools expected to conserve tradition or to foster change? Are they expected to reproduce the social and economic structure or to alter it? Are they expected to prepare people to meet the demands of the existing economic structures, or to enable the creation of different economic structures? These questions, stemming from the first of the three aspects of the cultural perspective on educational change correspond to the adaptive function of schools, or how they meet societal demands. Jerome Bruner summarizes this perspective well in this way:

> It is surely the case that schooling is only one small part of how a culture inducts the young into its canonical ways. Indeed, schooling may even be at odds with a culture's other ways of inducting the young into the requirements of communal living…. What has become increasingly clear… is that education is not just about conventional school matters like curriculum or standards or testing. What we resolve to do in school only makes sense when considered in the broader context of what the society intends to accomplish through its educational investment in the young. How one conceives of education, we have finally come to recognize, is a function of how one conceives of culture and its aims, professed and otherwise. (Bruner 1996, pp. ix–x)

Societies vary and experience periodic contention regarding the role of schools in the development of values among students, but there is less contention regarding the role of schools in helping students gain knowledge and skills. As the goals of curriculum broaden, as is the case when we develop intentional global education curriculum, this expansion activates discussions about the appropriate role for schools, and what should be off-limits for a public institution as it encroaches on the private domains of families or religious groups. Most people would agree that schools should teach students to read and computational thinking, but there's likely to be more contention regarding a climate change curriculum or a civic education curriculum that engages students in examining dilemmas reflected in government actions.

A core aspect of the cultural perspective on education is the balance that schools are expected to strive for between conserving and transforming social institutions. Schools balance a set of conservative norms, passing on to the young elements of culture what each generation agrees should be transmitted, as well as a set of transformative norms, passing on to the young a certain dissatisfaction with the present, and the desire to imagine and eventually build a new set of norms. From this latter viewpoint, schools are spaces that can anticipate a better society in the future, activating students' moral imagination, not just transmitting the social institutions of the present. Societies differ in the balance they expect their schools to achieve between conserving tradition and transforming society, and a cultural perspective in reforming education is about understanding those cultural expectations and boundaries, and aligning educational change to them or using the relative autonomy of schools to challenge those expectations.

A second aspect of a culture of education concerns how society views teachers and teaching. This cultural view about who should teach shapes who the teachers are at any given point in a society. Only on the basis of knowledge about what kind of professionals teachers are at any particular time in a given setting is it possible to design change in a way that works for them and with them and not over their heads. For instance, Singapore's reverence for its teachers is well documented, in contrast to contexts where teacher appointments are governed by patronage and corruption. Where teachers are respected as professionals, societies place greater trust in them to make choices in the interests of children. A process to introduce global education in a setting of highly professional teachers, such as Singapore, may not work in a context where teachers have very limited knowledge and skills, because teaching is not valued as a profession.

Also included in a cultural perspective on educational change is the notion that there is a culture of education, a set of shared norms and practices that define how instruction should be conducted. Ideas about how teacher or student-centered instruction should be, about whether education should consist of lectures or group work, about whether teachers should collaborate with their peers or work independently, and about the role students are expected to play in shaping the curriculum all should be factored in the design of a global education program. This culture of education is resilient, once crystalized into norms, artifacts, and practices it changes slowly, in part because it is challenging for teachers to teach in ways they themselves have not experienced. Efforts to advance global education programs in a school or in a system are, inevitably, efforts to transform the culture of education. Such a change does not happen overnight. The new knowledge and ideas that teachers gain as a result of professional development, or the new practices they are induced to enact through new curriculum, or through new forms of student or teacher assessment, have to be negotiated with pre-existing culture and norms. In a seminal study of the history of education reform in the United States, Tyack and Cuban argue that federal government policies arrive to schools as mandates which are layered on top of previous mandates, and that successive reform efforts form "geological layers" observable in the instructional practices in schools (Tyack and Cuban 1995, p. 76).

A corollary of adopting a cultural perspective is that education reform takes time, and therefore cycles of reform should be relatively long. Because every reform attempts to shape the culture of education negotiating the existing "geological layers" of previous reforms, it is necessary for the reform to stay the course until policy intentions find their way to instructional practice, and stay there long enough to become the new norms and shared meanings of how instruction is done. This process of learning new meanings and practices while "unlearning" pre-existing practices takes time, as it unfolds in the minds of individuals and in the negotiated social interactions among different individuals in school settings. Interrupting a reform before it has had a chance to crystalize into a system of new practices will not only result in little change, it will also undermine openness to further change in the future.

1.2 A Psychological Perspective on Educational Change

A psychological perspective highlights the implications of science-based knowledge about how people learn, for the process of teaching and learning, for students, teachers, and others supporting instruction. The core questions from a psychological point of view are: what should students learn when, how can they be supported in learning it, and what and how should teachers teach and how can they be supported in learning so they can teach effectively.

Since the early stages in the development of psychology as an independent science, many have argued that the scientific study of human functioning and development could help improve education. One of the early proponents of that thesis was Swiss psychologist Edouard Claparede, who proposed an experimental approach to education and created an institute to develop a science of education: the Rousseau Institute. The first directors, Pierre Bovet and his successor Jean Piaget, were also co-founders in 1925, with Claparede, of the International Bureau of Education (IBE), the first center of comparative education research. Once UNESCO was created, the IBE became part of the organization, serving as the entity that would translate educational scientific knowledge into programs and practices that it disseminated to support educational institutions around the world.

While it would seem evident that scientific knowledge about learning and instruction is necessary for a reform to be ultimately effective in helping students develop the intended global competencies, and that operational definitions and measurements of the desired competencies could help inform curriculum and pedagogy, the history of the relationship between psychology and education is a fractured one. David Olson argues that it is insufficient attention to the institutional nature of schools from psychologists which accounts for the fissure:

> A too sharp distinction between persons and institutions makes much good science irrelevant to the understanding of schooling, whereas conflating the two hides the effects of the schooling from our view, reducing it to just one more factor in personal and social development. (Olson 2003, p. xi)

The choice of which competencies should be included in the curriculum standards straddles the cultural perspective and the psychological perspective in that choosing which competencies to cultivate reflects normative choices resulting from cultural understandings about what is necessary as well as psychological knowledge about what is possible and helpful to individuals. An example of how psychology can characterize different educational objectives are Benjamin Bloom's taxonomies for knowledge-based, skills-based and affective educational goals. Bloom, an educational psychologist, argued that such goals could be construed as hierarchies reflecting increasing level of cognitive functioning. For knowledge, for example, Bloom's taxonomy encompassed knowledge, comprehension, application, analysis, synthesis, and evaluation (Bloom 1956).

Another example of a psychological perspective contribution to the definition of desired educational outcomes is the theory of multiple intelligences developed by Howard Gardner in which he argues that human potential can be characterized along eight domains, and not the more restricted domain which intelligence tests measured: linguistic, logical-mathematical, spatial, bodily kinesthetic, musical, interpersonal, intrapersonal, and naturalistic (Gardner 1983).

The Organization for Economic Cooperation and Development (OECD) undertook the Defining and Selecting Competencies project (DeSeCo) which drew on the contributions of psychology to categorize essential competencies, knowledge, and skills for a knowledge-based economy. Alongside this work, the OECD established the Program for International Student Assessment (PISA) a cross-national program to assess 15-year olds' knowledge and skills in literacy, mathematics, and science. Both DeSeCo and PISA also reflect a hierarchy of cognitive functioning.

The National Research Council of the United States assembled an expert group to synthesize existing knowledge about capacities that have value for life and work. Drawing on decades of mostly psychological research, the chairs of the group, Pellegrino and Hilton, synthesized those skills as follows in the report of the group (Pellegrino and Hilton 2012).

1. **Cognitive Skills**

    1.1. Processing and cognitive strategies

    - Critical Thinking
    - Problem Solving
    - Analysis
    - Logical Reasoning
    - Interpretation
    - Decision-Making
    - Executive Functioning

    1.2. Knowledge

    - Literacy and communication skills
    - Active listening skills
    - Knowledge of the disciplines
    - Ability to use evidence and assess biases in information
    - Digital Literacy

1.3. Creativity

- Creativity
- Innovation

2. **Interpersonal skills**

    2.1. Collaborative group skills

    - Communication
    - Collaboration
    - Teamwork
    - Cooperation
    - Coordination
    - Empathy, Perspective Taking
    - Trust
    - Service Orientation
    - Conflict Resolution
    - Negotiation

    2.2. Leadership

    - Leadership
    - Responsibility
    - Assertive Communication
    - Self-presentation
    - Social Influence

3. **Intra-personal skills**

    3.1. Intellectual Openness

    - Flexibility
    - Adaptability
    - Artistic and Cultural Appreciation
    - Personal and Social Responsibility
    - Intercultural competency
    - Appreciation for diversity
    - Adaptability
    - Capacity for lifelong learning
    - Intellectual interest and curiosity

    3.2. Work Ethic. Responsibility

    - Initiative
    - Self-direction
    - Responsibility
    - Perseverance
    - Productivity
    - Persistence

- Self-Regulation
- Meta-cognitive skills, anticipate future, reflexive skills
- Professionalism
- Ethics
- Integrity
- Citizenship
- Work Orientation

3.3. Self-efficacy

- Self-regulation (self-monitoring and self-assessment)
- Physical and mental health.

In addition to supporting the definition of the competencies which should be developed in schools, a psychological perspective also helps inform the design of the process through which teachers can help students gain such competencies. This is the role of a theory of learning and of an associated theory of teaching. Findings from cognitive science related to learning can help inform how to structure instruction so it is most effective. A recent synthesis of that research structures the key findings around the following key questions about learning (Deans for Impact 2015):

1. How do students understand new ideas?
    a. Students learn new ideas by reference to ideas they already know.
    b. To learn students must transfer information from working memory to long-term memory. Students have limited memory capacities that can be overwhelmed by tasks that are cognitively too demanding. Understanding new ideas can be impeded if students are confronted with too much information at once.
    c. Cognitive development does not progress through a fixed sequence of age-related stages. The mastery of new concepts happens in fits and starts.
2. How do students learn and retain new information?
    a. Information is often withdrawn from memory just at it went in. We usually want students to remember what information means and why it is important, so they should think about meaning when they encounter to-be-remembered material.
    b. Practice is essential to learning new facts, but not all practice is equivalent.
3. How do students solve problems?
    a. Each subject area has some sets of facts that, if committed to long-term memory, aids problem-solving by freeing working memory resources and illuminating contexts in which existing knowledge and skills can be applied. The size and content of this set vary by subject matter.
    b. Effective feedback is often essential to acquiring new knowledge and skills.
4. How does learning transfer to new situations in or outside of classrooms?
    a. The transfer of knowledge or skills to a novel problem requires both knowledge of the problem's context and a deep understanding of the problem's underlying structure.
    b. We understand new ideas via examples, but it is often hard to see the unifying underlying concepts in different examples.
5. What motivates students to learn?

a. Beliefs about intelligence are important predictors of student behavior in school.
   b. Self-determined motivation (a consequence of values or pure interest) leads to better long-term outcomes than controlled motivation (a consequence or reward/punishment or perceptions of self-worth).
   c. The ability to monitor their own thinking can help students identify what they do and do not know, but people are often unable to accurately judge their own learning and understanding.
   d. Students will be more motivated and successful in academic environments when they believe that they belong and are accepted in those environments.
6. What are common misconceptions about how students think and learn?
   a. Students do not have different "learning styles."
   b. Humans do not use only 10% of their brains.
   c. People are not preferentially "right-brained" or "left-brained" in the use of their brains.
   d. Novices and experts cannot think in all the same ways.
   e. Cognitive development does not progress via a fixed progression of age-related stages. (Deans for Impact 2015).

1.3 A Professional Perspective on Educational Change

A professional perspective focuses on the extent to which instruction is guided by expert knowledge, and supports relying on expertise as a foundation for practice. A professional perspective focuses on structuring the roles of education practitioners so that practice can be informed by expert knowledge and help generate such expert knowledge as a driver of change. The psychological perspective, the science of learning and teaching, can provide knowledge about how best to support instruction. The professional perspective, in contrast, focuses on the structure of roles and institutions which integrate such expert knowledge with practice. For instance, rules about who can teach, under what conditions, and with how much autonomy; criteria for teacher professional preparation and accreditation; norms for who can prepare teachers; and norms to guide the appointment and support the development of teacher careers. These are all instruments designed to constrain and support professional practice, and to align it with the deployment of expert-based knowledge.

The key questions from this perspective are, given a new set of curriculum objectives and expected pedagogies, what are the capacities necessary to teach this curriculum, and what is the gap between the current level of teacher capacities and those capacities which are necessary. The identification of this gap is then the foundation to create conditions to establish norms and support the professional development necessary to close the gap.

A tenet of this perspective is that it is essential to help teachers develop the professional mindsets and skills that enable them to deal with the many unexpected challenges they will encounter over their careers. Also important in this perspective is to provide education professionals with the necessary autonomy and voice to practice professionally. A subset of those ideas sees schools as learning organizations, which have the adaptive capacities to continuously professionalize teachers and leaders as they address emerging and unanticipated challenges, a theme which will be developed later in this book. A school as a learning organization is defined by several characteristics: (1) a shared vision centered on learning of all students, (2) continued learning opportunities for all staff, (3) team learning and collaboration among staff, (4) a culture of inquiry, innovation, and exploration, (5) embedded systems for collecting and exchanging knowledge and learning, (6) learning with and from the external environment and (7) modeling and growing learning leadership (Kools and Stoll 2016).

This perspective is reflected in the concept of "Professional capital" developed by Andy Hargreaves and Michael Fullan:

> Good teaching for all learners requires teachers to be highly committed, thoroughly prepared, continuously developed, properly paid, well networked with each other to maximize their own improvement, and able to make effective judgements using all their capabilities and experience. (Hargreaves and Fullan 2012, p. 3)

A professional perspective values not only the expertise and professional knowledge of practitioners, but more generally expert knowledge, hence research and evaluation are important elements in this view, as are instructional resources developed to reflect expertise and to support expert instructional practice.

Recognizing the level of professionalism of teachers in an education system at a given time is critical to determining the particular development efforts necessary to support them. For example, in a context in which teachers have been socialized to see their work primarily as transmitting content in a particular discipline, significant investments in professional development will be necessary for them to be able to lead instruction focused on project-based learning in collaboration with colleagues. Similarly, teachers with serious gaps in content knowledge will need more support to address those gaps than those who have been well prepared in the subjects they are to teach. In addition, in any given system there is likely great variation in the level of professionalization among teachers, so professional development must be responsive to such variation.

But it is not only the specifics of how to approach teacher professional development that should respond to the characteristics of teachers in a school or in a system, other structural elements of the "system" of education should also be aligned to the level of professionalization of the teacher. For example, greater school autonomy to design curriculum is desirable in schools where teachers are highly qualified, but not in schools where teachers have serious knowledge and skills gaps. Other elements of the education "system" need to be considered when we plan educational change, a subject to which we now turn.

1.4 An Institutional Perspective on Educational Change

An institutional perspective focuses on the educational structures, norms, regulations, incentives, and organizational design which provide stability and meaning to the work of teaching and learning and to all social interactions designed to support them (Scott 2004, 2008). These structures operate at various levels, nested within each other: the classroom in the school, the school in the district, the district in the state, and the state in the nation. The following definition of an education system provided by the Global Partnership for Education illustrates this perspective:

> Collections of institutions, actions and processes that affect the educational status of citizens in the short and long run. Education systems are made up of a large number of actors (teachers, parents, politicians, bureaucrats, civil society organizations) interacting with each other in different institutions (schools, ministry departments) for different reasons (developing curricula, monitoring school performance, managing teachers). All these interactions are governed by rules, beliefs and behavioral norms that affect how actors react and adapt to changes in the system. (Global Partnership for Education 2019, p. xvii)

The focus in this perspective is on the key elements and processes which define the "*system*" that supports instruction and on how to achieve internal coherence and alignment among the various elements which constitute a reform. An education "system" is structured by elements such as curriculum, instructional resources, school structure and buildings, governance, staff, assessments, and funding. From this perspective, education is a system, a bureaucracy, where organizational design and incentives can support the necessary instruction and learning, and it is important that these elements are coherent and well-aligned for optimal results. A curriculum fostering global education will do little to change the instructional core if it is not accompanied by adequate professional development and by student assessment systems which focus on those skills. Several scholars of education reform have argued that the failure of many education reforms is grounded in the inability of education reformers to understand schools as social institutions (Tyack and Tobin 1994; Tyack and Cuban 1995, p. 209; Olson 2003, p. 12).

A recent review of research on education reform in the United States argues, contrary to the most typical interpretations, that a number of reforms in fact succeeded at scale or in some "niche" or sub-system version, although the authors conclude that reform of instruction was more likely to succeed as a "niche" than system-wide effort and that curriculum reforms at scale failed. Offering an institutional explanation for the success of the reforms which were able to scale, the authors conclude that they did so because these reforms did not "require deep change in practice and extensive capacity building. They were adopted and implemented rapidly and widely in part because they could work within existing educational organization and culture. The unsuccessful cases of such reform typically did require deeper change in practice and more extensive capacity building, and so could not be scaled up easily or quickly" (Mehta and Cohen 2017, p. 646–647). The authors of the study identify five characteristics of education reforms which straddle an institutional and a political perspective:

1.4 An Institutional Perspective on Educational Change

> Our analysis suggests that there are at least five characteristics of successful educational reforms. First, some offered solutions to problems that the people who worked in or around education knew that they had and wanted to solve; they met felt needs for the people who would implement them. Second, some offered solutions that illuminated a real problem that educators had not been aware of, or couldn't figure out how to solve, but they embraced the reform once they saw or believed that it would help; these reforms illuminated a problem of practice and offered a solution. Third, some reforms succeeded because they satisfied demands that arose from the political, economic or social circumstances of schooling; these reforms worked because there was strong popular pressure on and/or in educational organizations or governments to accomplish some educational purpose. Four, in each of these cases, reforms also either offered the educational tools, materials, and practical guidance educators needed to put the reform into practice, or they helped educators to capitalize on existing tools, materials and guidance. Less difficult reforms required less capacity building while more ambitious reforms required more. Fifth, in a locally controlled and democratically governed system of schooling, successful reforms have been roughly consistent with the values of the educators, parents, and students they affected, though this worked differently in system wide than niche versions. (Mehta and Cohen 2017, p. 646)

A number of studies of "best practices" or "high performing systems" typically reflect this institutional perspective, focusing on practices, processes, structures, and norms which can help students perform at high levels.

For example, an OECD report drawing lessons for the United States from countries where students performed at high levels in PISA identified the following characteristics of high-performing systems:

1. A commitment to education and a belief that all students can achieve at high levels
2. Ambitious, focused and coherent education standards driving the system, aligned with instructional systems
3. Supporting capacity in schools
4. A work organization in which teachers can use their potential in terms of how the system is managed, accountability, and knowledge management
5. Institutionalizing improved instructional practice
6. Aligning incentive structures and engaging stakeholders
7. Complementing external accountability approaches with internal accountability to colleagues and parents
8. Investing resources where they have the greatest impact
9. Balancing local responsibility with capable central offices with the authority and legitimacy to act
10. Workplace training to support school-to-work transitions
11. Coherence of policies and practices, aligning policies across all elements of the system and ensuring coherence of policies over sustained periods of time
12. Ensuring openness of the system to the external environment to support continuous improvement (OECD 2011).

The Grattan Institute, a public policy think tank in Australia, produced a report identifying the following common characteristics of high-performing systems in East Asia:

1. High equity
2. Effective learning and teaching
3. Connecting policy to classroom learning
4. Focus on best practices
5. Emphasis on induction and mentoring
6. Developing teacher groups for research and classroom observation
7. Have career structures for teachers (Jensen 2012).

Similarly, the National Conference of State Legislatures in the United States, drawing on this comparative study of high-performing education systems, developed a seven-step protocol to build a world-class education system: build an inclusive team and set priorities, study and learn from top performers, create a shared statewide vision, benchmark policies, get started on one piece, work through "messiness," and invest the time (National Conference of State Legislatures 2016). The report identified four elements of a world-class education system:

- Children come to school ready to learn, and extra support is given to struggling students so that all have the opportunity to achieve high standards. [...]
- A world-class teaching profession supports a world-class instructional system, where every student has access to highly effective teachers and is expected to succeed. [...]
- A highly effective, intellectually rigorous system of career and technical education is available to those preferring an applied education. [...]
- Individual reforms are connected and aligned as parts of a clearly planned and carefully designed comprehensive system. (National Conference of State Legislatures 2016, p. 10).

Similarly, the National Center on Education and the Economy in the United States synthesized nine building blocks for world-class education systems, drawing on a comparative study of high-performing education systems (National Conference of State Legislatures 2016):

1. Provide strong support for children and their families before students arrive at school …
2. Provide more resources for at-risk students than for others …
3. Develop world-class, highly coherent instructional systems …
4. Create clear gateways for students through the system, set to global standards, with no dead ends …
5. Assure an abundant supply of highly qualified teachers …
6. Redesign schools to be places in which teachers will be treated as professionals, with incentives and support to continuously improve their professional practice and the performance of their students …
7. Create an effective system of career and technical education and training …
8. Create a leadership development system that develops leaders at all levels to manage such systems effectively …
9. Institute a governance system that has the authority and legitimacy to develop coherent, powerful policies and is capable of implementing them at scale (National Conference of State Legislatures 2016, pp. 7–13).

1.5 A Political Perspective on Educational Change

A political perspective recognizes that education affects the interests of many different groups, and that those interests vary within and across groups, and may be in conflict with one another. As examples of variation within groups, students and parents are key stakeholders of the education system, the presumed beneficiaries of education, but not all students or parents have the same interests with respect to reform. For example, the parents of students with disabilities might value reforms that promote inclusive education more than those who don't have the same needs, the parents of children who speak indigenous languages may value policies of bilingual education differently than the parents of children who speak the dominant language, and the parents of low income children may value compensatory education policies differently than the more socioeconomically advantaged parents. Interests vary also among groups. Teachers are also a group with interests in education, and those interests may not fully coincide with those of students. The same is true of elected public officials, government bureaucrats, teacher organizations, and business groups that provide services to schools or hire school graduates. Pivotal in a political perspective of education is understanding how education politics relate to national politics. In some settings, education organizations are more loosely coupled than in others to national political parties and to national politics. In some contexts, the position of particular education actors with respect to educational change issues, such as teacher unions and government officials, are subsidiary to the relationship between political groups at the national level.

Whereas the institutional and professional perspectives either assume congruence among the interests of various stakeholders of education reform or prioritize the interests of one group over others, a political perspective recognizes the potential for conflicting interests among stakeholders and sees reform as a way to resolve those conflicts. The key questions in this perspective are how to ascertain the position of various stakeholder groups with respect to a reform, and how to move all of them to negotiate their interests so they can be more supportive of the reform, while also managing or overpowering those groups who oppose it.

Some argue that political interests are so powerful in shaping educational institutions and practice, that they can override the educational interests of students. Based on a study of the academic achievement of 60,000 students from low income families in 1,015 private and public schools in the United States, and on a series of case studies of turnaround schools, Chubb and Moe argue that public education does not serve disadvantaged groups, that overall public schools fail to provide students opportunities to develop the competencies the economy demands, and that private schools exhibit superior performance because they are accountable to parents (Chubb and Moe 1990).

A recent World Bank report on education argues that it is often politics which explain the lack of alignment between the key elements in an education system, and that a successful reform strategy requires mobilizing stakeholders so that they support the alignment of those elements with learning. The report explains that those key stakeholders with influence over learners, teachers, school inputs and management, and who often pull those key elements of the system away from learning, include politicians, civil society organizations, peers and communities, the judiciary, the private sector, bureaucrats, international actors, and other actors. In order to make the system work for learning these actors need to be aligned so their actions support learning. (World Bank 2018, p. 21).

> But education systems can have other goals that can hamper efforts to improve learning. For example, politicians sometimes view education systems as a tool for rewarding their supporters with civil service jobs, or for impressing voters with school construction programs that are visible but not strategically planned. These goals can be misaligned with learning, leaving schools with building they cannot use and teachers who are not proficient. Where these goals compete with other goals, the result is that the overall education system and its actors are not aligned toward learning. (World Bank 2018, p. 175)

To sum up, the process of educational change is not just a cultural process, which it is, or a psychological, or professional, or institutional, or political process. It is all of the above, and a useful theory should help understand its multidimensionality. Together, these five perspectives illuminate the complete process of change as the partial elements highlighted by each perspective offers a perspective that complements what other perspectives enlighten and, together, these various elements brought to light by each perspective interact with the elements highlighted by other perspectives (Reimers 2020). Paraphrasing Goethe who said that the person who speaks with only one language sees the world with one eye, thinking about educational change through a singular frame is seeing change with one eye. A multidimensional model thus helps capture the gestalt of the process of educational change and provides depth, perspective, a fuller, and more complete understanding.

References

Bloom, B. S. (1956). *Taxonomy of educational objectives*. Boston, MA: Published by Allyn and Bacon.
Bolman, L., & Deal, T. (1991). *Reframing organizations. Artistry, choice and leadership*. Wiley.
Bruner, J. (1996). *The culture of education*. Cambridge, MA: Harvard University Press.
Chubb, J., & Moe, T. (1990). *Politics, markets and America's schools*. Washington, DC: Brookings Institutions.
Davies, I., Ho, L. C., Kiwan, D., Peck, C. L., Peterson, A., Sant, E., et al. (Eds.). (2018). *The Palgrave handbook of global citizenship and education*. London, UK: Palgrave Macmillan.
Deans for Impact. (2015). *The science of learning*. Austin, TX: Deans for Impact.
Elmore, R. (1996). Getting to scale with good educational practice. *Harvard Educational Review, 66*(1), 1–27.
Foundation, Longview. (2008). *Teacher preparation for the global age*. Silver Spring, MD: Longview Foundation.
Gardner, H. (1983). *Frames of mind: The theory of multiple intelligences*. New York: Basic Books.
Global Partnership for Education. (2019). *Country level evaluations. Synthesis report*. Retrieved January 23, 2020, from https://www.globalpartnership.org/content/synthesis-report-gpe-country-level-evaluations-february-2019.
Hargreaves, A., & Fullan, M. (2012). *Professional capital*. New York: Teachers College Press.

References

Jensen, B. (2012). *Catching up: Learning from the best school systems in East Asia: Summary report*. Melbourne, Australia: Grattan Institute.

Klein, J. (2016). *Global education guidebook: Humanizing K-12 classrooms worldwide through equitable partnerships* (How to promote multicultural education and nurture global citizens). Bloomington, IN: Solution Tree Press.

Kools, M., & Stoll, L. (2016). *What makes a school a learning organization* (OECD. Directorate of Education and Skills, Education Working Paper No. 137). Paris: OECD.

Lewin, K. (1952). *Field theory in social science: Selected theoretical papers by Kurt Lewin*. London: Tavistock

Mehta, J., & Cohen, D. (2017). Why reform sometime succeeds: Understanding the conditions that produce reforms that last. *American Educational Research Journal, 54*(4), 644–690.

National Conference of State Legislatures. (2016). *No time to lose: How to build a world-class education system state by state*.

OECD. (2011). *Strong performers and successful performers in education: Lessons from PISA for the United States*. Paris: OECD.

OECD. (2019d). *PISA 2018 results. What school life means for student life* (Vol. 3). Retrieved December 6, 2019, from https://www.oecd.org/pisa/.

OECD and Asia Society. (2018). *Teaching for global competence in a rapidly changing world*. Paris: OECD. https://asiasociety.org/sites/default/files/inline-files/teaching-for-global-competence-in-a-rapidly-changing-world-edu.pdf.

Olson, D. (2003). *Psychological theory and educational reform*. Cambridge: Cambridge University Press.

Pellegrino, J. W., & Hilton, M. L. (Eds.). (2012). *Education for life and work: Developing transferable knowledge and skills in the 21st century*. Washington, DC: The National Academies Press.

Reimers, F. (2020). *Audacious education purposes*. Springer (in press).

Scheerens, J. (2000). *Improving school effectiveness*. International Institute for Educational Planning: UNESCO.

Scott, W. R. (2004). Institutional theory. In G. Ritzer (Ed.) *Encyclopedia of social theory* (pp. 407–414). Thousand Oaks, CA: Sage.

Scott, W. R. (2008). *Institutions and organizations: Ideas and interests*. Los Angeles, CA: Sage.

Tavangar, H. S., & Mladic-Morales, B. (2014). *The global education toolkit for elementary learnings*. Thousand Oaks, CA: Corwin.

Tyack, D., & Tobin, W. (1994). The 'grammar' of schooling: why has it been so hard to change? *American Educational Research Journal, 31*(3), 452–479.

Tyack, D., & Cuban, L. (1995). *Tinkering towards Utopia. A century of public school reform*. Cambridge, MA: Harvard University Press.

UNESCO (1974) *Recommendation concerning education for international understanding, co-operation and peace and education relating to human rights and fundamental freedoms*. 19 November 1974.

UNESCO (2015) *Not just hot air. Putting climate change education into practice*.

UNESCO. (2017). *Education for sustainable development goals learning objectives*. Paris: UNESCO.

UNESCO. (2018). *Progress on education for sustainable development and global citizenship education: Findings of the 6th consultation on the implementation of the 1974 recommendation concerning education for international understanding*. Retrieved January 23, 2020, from https://unesdoc.unesco.org/ark:/48223/pf0000266176.

UNESCO. (2019). *Education for sustainable development*. Retrieved January 23, 2020, from https://en.unesco.org/themes/education-sustainable-development.

United Nations. (2020). Sustainable development goals. Retrieved January 23, 2020, from https://www.un.org/sustainabledevelopment/education/.

Vansteenkiste, M., & Sheldon, K. (2006) There's nothing more practical than a good theory: Integrating motivational interviewing and self-determination theory. British journal of clinical psychology 45(1), 63–82. The British Psychological Society.

World Bank. (2018). *Learning to realize education's promise*. Washington, DC: World Bank.

Open Access This chapter is licensed under the terms of the Creative Commons Attribution 4.0 International License (http://creativecommons.org/licenses/by/4.0/), which permits use, sharing, adaptation, distribution and reproduction in any medium or format, as long as you give appropriate credit to the original author(s) and the source, provide a link to the Creative Commons license and indicate if changes were made.

The images or other third party material in this chapter are included in the chapter's Creative Commons license, unless indicated otherwise in a credit line to the material. If material is not included in the chapter's Creative Commons license and your intended use is not permitted by statutory regulation or exceeds the permitted use, you will need to obtain permission directly from the copyright holder.

Chapter 2
What Is Global Education and Why Does It Matter?

Global education are both practices guided by a set of purposes and approaches intentionally created to provide opportunities for students to develop global competencies, and the theories that explain and inform those practices and their effects. Global competencies encompass the knowledge, skills, and dispositions that help students develop, understand, and function in communities which are increasingly interdependent with other communities around the world, and that provide a foundation for lifelong learning of what they need to participate, at high levels of functioning, in environments in continuous flux because of increasing global change.

A competence encompasses more than knowledge and skills "It involves the ability to meet complex demands, by drawing on and mobilizing psychosocial resources (including skills and attitudes) in a particular context. For example, the ability to communicate effectively is a competency that may draw on an individual's knowledge of language, practical IT skills, and attitudes towards those with whom he or she is communicating" (OECD 2005, p. 4).

A quintessentially global topic is climate change. Global competency should enable people to understand climate change, to adapt to mitigate its impact, and hopefully to revert it. Climate Change Education, a subdomain of Education for Sustainable Development, is a modality of Global Education focused on preparing people to achieve more sustainable ways to relate to our habitat. It encompasses preparation to adopt practices that are known to be sustainable, for example slowing down population growth, consuming a diet with a smaller carbon footprint, or using renewable energies. These practices may be individual in the choices we make about our own consumption and lifestyle, or they may be collective, the result of choices we make as citizens when we participate in the democratic process in various levels of government or when we influence the behavior of corporations. Government policies are essential to slowing global warming, and they are subject to influence and preferences by citizens, educated to understand the scientific consensus on climate change and with the capacity to exercise influence as citizens.

But Climate Change Education encompasses also the development of the innovation skills necessary to slow down climate change, which requires advancing knowledge and inventing technologies that can help us transform our interactions with the

© The Author(s) 2020
F. M. Reimers, *Educating Students to Improve the World*,
SpringerBriefs in Education, https://doi.org/10.1007/978-981-15-3887-2_2

environment, in a way reinvent our way of life. As a result, educating to mitigate climate change and for sustainability involves equipping people with the necessary skills for such advancement of knowledge and invention.

An example from the field of sanitation will illustrate the role of inventive skills in addressing climate change. In his efforts to improve sanitation in the developing world, Bill Gates concluded that the toilets and water treatment systems developed and in use in the early industrialized world were poor fits to developing countries because they were resource-intensive and generated excessive waste. This caused him to undertake projects to stimulate innovation in the design of next-generation toilets that could operate without sewer systems (Brueck 2019; D'Agostino 2018).

The competencies gained from global education should help students understand how the communities in which they live relate to other communities around the world, how they are affected from that interaction and affect others, how their lives are shaped by topics which are global in nature, such as climate change, or trade, or scientific cooperation, and to participate in forms of global action and cooperation within their spheres of influence in ways which contribute effectively to the various communities they are a part of, and in this way improving the world.

There are different intellectual traditions that influence how global education is defined and conceptualized. These perspectives draw on various intellectual traditions: globalism, nationalism, internationalism, transnationalism, cosmopolitanism, post-colonialism, and indigeneity. They are anchored in diverse core concepts: justice, equity, diversity, identity and belonging, and sustainable development. They include perspectives that accept the existing international social and economic order, along with others that are more critical (Davies et al. 2018).

Following a cosmopolitanist and critical perspective, in my own work developing global citizenship curriculum, I have adopted the United Nations Sustainable Development Goals as a guiding framework because they articulate a capacious vision of sustainability and because they tie global education as a theoretical field and practice to a set of concepts that are widely shared across many fields of human endeavor, including education, but extending also into public health, work and industry, poverty alleviation, environmental sustainability, poverty reduction. These seventeen goals are deeply rooted in multiple disciplines focused on human and social development. The Sustainable Development Goals pose also a challenge to the very notions of development and social progress, emphasizing the interdependence of inclusion, social justice, peace and environmental sustainability (Reimers et al. 2016, 2017).

Global education encompasses the traditional disciplines in service of helping students understand the world in which they live: sciences, social sciences, and humanities. For example, to understand climate change it is necessary to understand the processes that explain how climate works, a subject of scientific study. A global education includes also opportunities for students to imagine and enact strategies to advance human well-being, which draws on the capacities of invention and ethical reasoning. This might include helping students to develop the curiosity to advance scientific understanding in a particular domain, or the desire to create products or services that advance well-being or solve problems, as with the previous example of reinventing toilets to address sanitation and advancing health.

Global education is not necessarily an additional curriculum domain, rather, it is a set of clear purposes which can help align the entire curriculum with real world questions, challenges, and opportunities. As such, global education is a way to help teachers as well as students understand the relationship between what is learned in school and the world outside the school. Global education encompasses also a series of approaches, pedagogies, curricula, and structures to support such instruction that is explicitly designed to help build the breadth of skills that can help students function in a deeply interdependent and increasingly globally integrated world. The Australian Curriculum Corporation defines it as follows:

> Global education is defined as an approach to education which seeks to enable young people to participate in shaping a better shared future for the world through: Emphasising the unity and interdependence of human society, Developing a sense of self an appreciation of cultural diversity, Affirming social justice and human rights, peace building and actions for a sustainable future, Emphasising developing relationships with our global neighbours, Promoting open-mindedness and a predisposition to take action for change. (Curriculum Corporation 2008, p. 2)

Global education includes multiple specific domains, such as environmental education and education for sustainability, understanding global affairs, understanding the process of globalization and of global interdependence, developing intercultural competency, fostering civic engagement, human rights, and peace education. Sciences and humanities are the disciplinary foundations of global education, for there is no way to understand the world without the knowledge, skills, and dispositions that result from learning to think as scientists do or reason as humanists can do.

For example, in order to understand climate change, students need to know not just the scientific consensus on the causes of climate change, but the underlying processes that are the major drivers of climate change producing significant release of carbon dioxide and other bases into the atmosphere which trap heat. Scientists have identified boundaries for ten systems within which humans and other species can live: freshwater use, land use, phosphorous pollution, ocean acidification, climate change, ozone depletion, nitrogen pollution, biodiversity loss, aerosol air, and chemical pollution. These systems are: ocean acidification, climate change, ozone depletion, nitrogen pollution, and biodiversity loss. Only after they understand those systems will students be able to comprehend the metrics which demonstrate the nature and causes of climate change. For eight of those system metrics for which we have data to compare pre-industrial revolution levels to current levels, five of them exceed the boundaries representing high risk that life is not sustainable. Furthermore, the remaining three metrics: freshwater use, land use, and phosphorous pollution, have changed significantly, in the direction of the increasing risk boundary. Only two of the eight metrics (ocean acidification and ozone depletion) have current values that are lower than the values before the industrial revolution (UNESCO 2017, p. 20). Only once they can understand those systems and metrics, will students be able to understand the scientific consensus which is that the main causes of those changes are human–environmental interactions, resulting from overpopulation, modern lifestyles and individual behavior (NASA 2020). But, as explained earlier, in order to contribute to the mitigation of climate change, students will need more than the scientific understanding of how climate works. They will need the capacity for systemic thinking, and the capacity to identify various criteria, value-based systems, to choose among alternatives and weigh tradeoffs among alternatives, so they can evaluate the costs and benefits involved in reducing population growth, or consumption, or in building circular economies with industries located closer to cities as a way to reduce transportation costs.

An effective program of global education is not the additive result of a series of isolated experiences in various curriculum silos, but the result of coherent and integrated learning opportunities that can help students understand the relationship between what they learn in various grades and subjects in service of understanding the world and of being able to act to improve it. As such, a global education helps students think about complexity and understand the systems which undergird global issues and global interdependence.

The Asia Society and the OECD define global competence as follows:

> Both OECD and the Center for Global Education have identified four key aspects of global competence. Globally competent youth: (1) investigate the world beyond their immediate environment by examining issues of local, global, and cultural significance; (2) recognize, understand, and appreciate the perspectives and world views of others; (3) communicate ideas effectively with diverse audiences by engaging in open, appropriate, and effective interactions across cultures; and (4) take action for collective well-being and sustainable development both locally and globally. (OECD and Asia Society 2018, p. 12)

A global education, in short, helps prepare students to live so that "nothing human is foreign to them" to quote the playwright Terence who expressed this cosmopolitan aspiration two thousand years ago, a quote that so captivated the sixteenth-century philosopher and humanist Michel de Montaigne that he engraved it in one of the beams of his study. Montaigne's focus on understanding human nature influenced many subsequent philosophers and scientists, including Rousseau, Bacon, Pascal, Descartes, and Emerson. He translated his humanist and cosmopolitan vision into ideas about how children should be educated. He argued that the goal of education was to prepare students for life and that this required experiential learning and personalization (Montaigne 1575).

In the chapters that follow, I explain each of these five perspectives in greater detail, illustrating how they can help approach the design and implementation of a program of global education.

References

Brueck, H. (2019). A $350 toilet powered by worms may be the ingenious future of sanitation that Bill Gates has been dreaming about. *Business Insider*.

Curriculum Corporation. (2008). *Global perspectives: A framework for global education in Australian Schools*. Carlton South, VC: Curriculum Corporation.

D'Agostino, R. (2018). How does Bill Gates's ingenious, waterless, life-saving toilet work? *Popular Mechanics*. https://www.popularmechanics.com/science/health/a24747871/bill-gates-life-saving-toilet/.

References

Davies, I., Ho, L. C., Kiwan, D., Peck, C. L., Peterson, A., Sant, E., et al. (Eds.). (2018). *The Palgrave handbook of global citizenship and education*. London, UK: Palgrave Macmillan.

Montaigne, M. (1575). *On the education of children*. http://essays.quotidiana.org/montaigne/education_of_children/.

NASA. (2020). *Global climate change. Vital signs of the planet*. Retrieved from January 14, 2020, from https://climate.nasa.gov/.

OECD. (2005). *Definition and selection of key competencies: Executive summary*. Paris: OECD. https://www.oecd.org/pisa/35070367.pdf.

OECD and Asia Society. (2018). *Teaching for global competence in a rapidly changing world*. Paris: OECD. https://asiasociety.org/sites/default/files/inline-files/teaching-for-global-competence-in-a-rapidly-changing-world-edu.pdf.

Reimers, F., Chopra, V., Chung, C., Higdon, J., & O'Donnell, E. B. (2016). *Empowering global citizens*. Charleston, SC: CreateSpace.

Reimers, F., et al. (2017). *Empowering students to improve the world in sixty lessons*. Charleston, SC: CreateSpace.

UNESCO. (2017). *Education for people and planet* (Global education monitoring report). Paris: UNESCO.

Open Access This chapter is licensed under the terms of the Creative Commons Attribution 4.0 International License (http://creativecommons.org/licenses/by/4.0/), which permits use, sharing, adaptation, distribution and reproduction in any medium or format, as long as you give appropriate credit to the original author(s) and the source, provide a link to the Creative Commons license and indicate if changes were made.

The images or other third party material in this chapter are included in the chapter's Creative Commons license, unless indicated otherwise in a credit line to the material. If material is not included in the chapter's Creative Commons license and your intended use is not permitted by statutory regulation or exceeds the permitted use, you will need to obtain permission directly from the copyright holder.

Chapter 3
A Cultural Perspective and Global Education

A cultural perspective on global education asks: how are the development of global awareness and competence relevant to the demands of society? Why should global education be a goal worth pursuing? The answer to this question is twofold. In many ways, education was always meant to be cosmopolitan, to empower students to understand and improve the world. But the velocity of change taking place around us, and the urgency to address the shared challenges we face as a planet, requires us to pursue with greater intentionality and effectiveness an education that is truly global. Clearly, there is a diversity of perspectives and intellectual traditions from which these questions can be answered (Davies et al. 2018). The perspective adopted here traces the roots of global education to old cosmopolitan aspirations, and discusses the evolution to contemporary shared challenges that require global collaboration and global citizenship not just to understand a world that is increasingly integrated, but also to improve it by making it more inclusive and sustainable, as suggested in the United Nations Sustainable Development Goals.

Many parents understand this urgency to increase the relevance of schools. Over 90% of Americans see global education as key to preparing children for the twenty-first century (NAFSA 2003). At the same time, paradoxically, however, one of the responses to globalization includes new manifestations of tribalism which challenge these cosmopolitan aspirations of global education.

3.1 The Long Roots of Global Education

The question of what goals should animate the efforts to educate students is as old as the first educational institutions in many different societies and civilizations. Educational institutions exist to serve a variety of purposes and it is with respect to those purposes that it is possible to make decisions about how to educate. For most of human history, the purpose of educational institutions was to educate only some members of society, typically those expected to take on some type of leadership positions, either political, religious, or administrative. Some cosmopolitan aspirations date from this

© The Author(s) 2020
F. M. Reimers, *Educating Students to Improve the World*,
SpringerBriefs in Education, https://doi.org/10.1007/978-981-15-3887-2_3

early period. Montaigne's ideas in the sixteenth century that education should prepare for an engaged, cosmopolitan life, exemplify this view. The very idea that all should be educated so we could have peace, expressed in the seventeenth century by John Amos Comenius, a Moravian Minister, conveys a similar aspiration that education should aim to help us find a shared humanity with others to avert conflict (Piaget 1993).

But as the idea that schools should educate many, perhaps all, of the younger members of a society took hold and led to the creation of national systems of education in the eighteenth century in Europe, questions of purpose resurfaced with new urgency. Because the idea that all people should be educated was a product of the Enlightenment, the philosophical movement that proposed that people were capable of ruling themselves and fundamentally equal, public education was from the outset meant to empower students to understand the world, and to transform it. One of the seminal philosophers of the enlightenment, Jean Jacques Rousseau, advocated in his treaty on education *Emile* that children should be the center of the educational process, and the development of autonomy and self-reliance are the chief goals of education. Rousseau saw the roots of politics in the educational process, and he considered his book on the social contract an appendix to his treaty on education (Soetard 1994a).

The Enlightenment was itself a cosmopolitan project, one of its key figures, Immanuel Kant, argued that accepting universal rights for all people would lead to peace:

> The social relations between the various peoples of the world have now advanced everywhere so far that a violation of Right in one place of the earth, is felt all over it… A Cosmo-political Rights of the whole Human Race, … is a necessary completion of the unwritten Code which carries national and international Right to a consummation in the Public Right of Mankind. Thus the whole system leads to the conclusion of a Perpetual Peace among the Nations. (Kant 1795, p. 24)

Enlightenment thinkers placed great hope in human reason and in science, as the faculty and the discipline that would help people understand the world. Consequently, public education was conceived as a way to cultivate human reason and access to science.

The oldest public education system, established in Prussia, had just those very goals, as reported by John Quincy Adams, a diplomat and the sixth president of the United States. Adams published a series of observations of the schools in Prussia in his book "Letters on Silesia" in which he described for his contemporaries in Boston how these institutions had been set up and funded. In particular, in a letter written in Berlin, dated March 7, 1801, Adams describes admiringly the success of Frederick the II, who ruled Prussia from 1740 until 1786, in instituting a system of publicly funded schools to educate all children, for the purpose of teaching them to read and introduce them to science. In his letters, Adams explained how the spread of literacy increased the circulation of newspapers, which would serve as avenues of lifelong learning. In order to spread literacy, the institutions of education had to be developed, and he also described how providing schoolmasters with a public wage, enabled the creation of schools for elementary instruction of all classes of people, and how the creation of the public school drove the search for specialized preparation for schoolmasters, so they could become more effective teaching all classes of students to read. In response to this need for specialized and effective training, Adams reports, an Augustine monk, Felbiger, devised an effective method of instruction which was disseminated at these normal schools to prepare teachers. Adams talks admiringly about Frederick the II, "the greatest general of his age, eminent as a writer in the highest departments of literature, descending, in a manner to teach the alphabet to the children of his kingdom, bestowing his care, his persevering assiduity, his influence and his power, in diffusing plain and useful knowledge among his subjects, in opening to their minds the first and most important pages of the book of science" (Adams 1804, p. 371–372).

Deeply influenced by Rousseau's work, Johan Pestalozzi, began a series of educational experiments to educate poor children, which combined education with work. Pestalozzi argued that children were not little adults and that education should be tailored to the stage of development of the learner (Soetard 1994b).

Public education was cosmopolitan not only in its aspiration to advance the goals of the enlightenment—of preparing citizens who could rule themselves and improve the world depending on reason and science—but also in that it benefits from cross-border collaborations, as people exchanged ideas and supported each other's efforts to build the twin institutions of public schools and democracy. The letters which John Quincy Adams wrote from Silesia, to inspire his readers in the newly independent United States of America, describing the Prussian education system exemplify such cosmopolitan nature of educational expansion.

About the same time as that when John Quincy Adams was writing admiringly in Silesia of Frederick II's efforts to establish a public education system to educate all children, Marc Antoine Jullien, a French journalist, politician, and diplomat, was writing in Paris about some of the key ideas about educational purposes and methods which existed in this time as public education systems were being established in Europe. Jullien studied the perspectives on the aims of education of two leading educators at the time: Johann Pestalozzi and Joseph Lancaster (Jullien 1812). Pestalozzi created an institute in Burgdorf Switzerland committed to offering students a rich curriculum for the purpose of fostering the development of a wide range of capacities (Soetard 1994b). Jullien corresponded frequently with Pestalozzi and sent three of his children to study at one of his institutes. Joseph Lancaster, in turn, had created an approach to educate all children at low cost, the monitorial method of instruction, in a more limited range of capacities. The free elementary school Lancaster established in Southwark, England in 1798 served as the laboratory to develop the method he would describe in his book *Improvements in Education*, published in 1803. Jullien became a promoter of the monitorial system of education Lancaster had devised. So enthused was Jullien with the promise of such systematic study of various educational approaches to help inform questions of educational purpose that he proposed a systematic survey of how schools were organized in diverse jurisdictions. He also organized the documentation and exchange of diverse education approaches and developed proposals for the organization of public education (Jullien 1817a, 1835, 1842). He shared his education publications with political leaders of his time, including Thomas Jefferson (Jullien 1817b).

As public education expanded across the world, learning from the experience of others in the enterprise of establishing public schools became one of the strategies of those leading such expansion. In the United States, for example, Horace Mann, the first secretary of education of Massachusetts, wrote a report based on a study tour of Germany and France in 1843 to examine their education systems which was pivotal in his campaign to establish public education in the State (Mann 1844). Similarly, Domingo Faustino Sarmiento, the first person to propose a public education system for the emerging independent republics in South America, did so after a study tour of the education systems in Europe and a visit to Boston to meet Horace Mann and discuss his ideas for the *Common School* (Sarmiento 1849).

It was such exchanges of ideas about how to educate all children that assisted the remarkable expansion of access to education which took place over the last century. Because of the cross-national and cosmopolitan nature of such exchanges, cosmopolitan ideas about the purposes of education were transferred as part of the process.

This cosmopolitan nature of exchanges about the aims of education was particularly visible in the transnational process of global collaboration to educate all children in the world which resulted from the inclusion of education in the Universal Declaration of Human Rights. Adopted in December of 1948 by the newly created United Nations, article 26 of the Universal Declaration of Human Rights, the propeller of the educational expansion which took place in the twentieth century, describes that right in this way:

> (1) Everyone has the right to education. Education shall be free, at least in the elementary and fundamental stages. Elementary education shall be compulsory. Technical and professional education shall be made generally available and higher education shall be equally accessible to all on the basis of merit.
>
> (2) Education shall be directed to the full development of the human personality and to the strengthening of respect for human rights and fundamental freedoms. It shall promote understanding, tolerance and friendship among all nations, racial or religious groups, and shall further the activities of the United Nations for the maintenance of peace.
>
> (3) Parents have a prior right to choose the kind of education that shall be given to their children. (UN 1948)

In declaring that all have the right to elementary education, the article states that education should be directed to the full development of human personality (as Johann Pestalozzi had proposed two centuries earlier in Switzerland) and in particular to the ethical goals of "strengthening respect for human rights and fundamental freedoms… promot[ing] understanding, tolerance and friendship among all nations, racial or religious groups…" (United Nations 1948).

The inclusion of the right to education in the Universal Declaration, and the establishment of UNESCO, the specialized United Nations agency to promote education, science, and culture, are manifestations of the cosmopolitan nature of the process of extending public education to all. Through these acts, the creation of the conditions that extend education to all became a shared responsibility of humanity, an expression of a global collective commitment to all children in the world. What could be more

3.1 The Long Roots of Global Education

cosmopolitan than this statement that the education of all of the world's children is now a shared enterprise of all citizens of the world?

Initially, global collaboration to educate all proceeded in the form of intergovernmental cooperation, but increasingly also through actions of various groups of civil society engaging ordinary citizens in these efforts. The adoption of the declaration, and of the universal right to education, had the effect of animating and supporting governments in significantly advancing access to education for all. In 1945, before the establishment of UNESCO, the world's population stood at 2.5 billion, of which less than half had any access to school. Seven decades later, with a world population at 7.5 billion, 85% had some access to school (Roser and Ortiz-Ospina 2019).

The creation of the United Nations and of UNESCO were key to advance global education around the world. Three efforts stand out in UNESCO's history producing documents that would respond to important global imperatives and advocate for global education in the context of offering ideas about how to educate for the future. By the end of the 1960s, educational access had increased significantly over the previous two decades. Such expansion was bringing about new questions about the goals of education.

In 1970, in response to a mandate of UNESCO's General Conference, which convened all education ministers from member states, the organization's director general asked Edgar Faure, a former Minister of Education of France, to head an international commission to prepare a report on the future of education. The report, of decidedly humanist inspiration, put forth the idea that the fundamental goal of education should be to prepare students to be lifelong learners, as the commission anticipated a future of accelerating change and of growing expectations of economic and political participation from people (Faure et al. 1972). The ambitious goal of preparing students for lifelong learning opened up conversations around the world about which capacities would equip people for such a task.

This report was followed with the International Recommendation concerning Education for International Understanding, Co-operation and Peace and Education relating to Human Rights and Fundamental freedoms which UNESCO proposed to member states in 1974.

Twenty years later, UNESCO's director general asked former European Commission chairman Jacques Delors to head a commission that would draft another global manifesto proposing directions for education. The result of a massive effort of global consultations spanning three years, the Delors Report, published in 1996, proposed an integrated vision of education anchored on the concept of "learning throughout life" and on four goals for education, learning to know, to do, to be and to live together (Delors 1996). That report too sparked global conversations about the need for a broader and more ambitious set of goals that should animate government's efforts in educating all children.

3.2 Growing Interest in Global Education

The publication of the Delors report reflected and animated a renewed interest in revisiting the goals of education in countries around the world. At a time of growing global interdependence, this revision led to an embracing of cosmopolitan aspirations for global education. This is most explicitly reflected in Delors' goal of "learning to live together."

A year after the Delors report was published, and as national and global conversations began to adopt its recommendations to think more ambitiously about what human capacities schools should develop, the Organization for Economic Cooperation and Development (OECD) launched an undertaking that would lead to greater operational clarity with regards to such capacities, the Definition and Selection of Competencies Project (known as the DeSeCo Project). The result of this expert consultation was to identify key competencies and help define overarching goals for education systems and lifelong learning (Rychen and Salganik 2001, 2003). DeSeCo identified as key competencies: interacting in socially heterogeneous groups, acting autonomously and using tools interactively. Each competency has an internal structure comprising various domains, for instance, the ability to cooperate encompasses: knowledge, cognitive skills, practical skills, attitudes, emotions, values and ethics and motivation related to cooperation (Rychen and Salganik 2003, p 44). DeSeCo is itself a cross-national collaboration that engages with the question of the common values and demands that justify the elaboration of a universal taxonomy of competencies:

> For our purpose (i.e., defining and selecting key competencies for a successful life and a well-functioning society), the assumed common values and the widespread acceptance of the international conventions means that universal objectives such as respect for human rights and sustainable development do exist and can serve as a regulative ideal and normative anchoring point for the discourse on key competencies. (Rychen 2003, p. 70–71)

The Delors Report, the DeSeCo Project, and similar national efforts undertaken in various countries to revisit what capacities would be necessary to participate in a rapidly changing world influenced governments to revisit national standards and curriculum frameworks. Complementing those efforts, OECD's Program of International Student Assessment (PISA), initiated at about the same time as the DeSeCo project, generated further interest in the definition and measurement of the knowledge and skills students around the world had gained by the age of fifteen. These efforts implicitly recognized that countries around the world should collaborate in defining which competencies should be developed in schools.

Similar efforts to re-examine the goals of education took place around the world as the result of technological and social changes. For example in 1981 the US Secretary of Education established a commission to review the quality of education in the country. The report, which recommended that schools should develop the skills that enabled the creation of a learning society, focused on content and skills. Among others, these emphasized foreign languages and cross-cultural communication skills (US National Commission on Excellence in Education 1983).

3.2 Growing Interest in Global Education

Ten years later, in 1991, the United States Department of Labor established a commission to define which competencies would be necessary given the changing nature of work. The report repeatedly refers to the growing demands for an expanded set of skills in an economy ever more globally interdependent. It also calls for national standards defining five competencies and three foundational skills. According to the report, the competencies that workers would require are the capacity to productively use resources, interpersonal skills, information, systems, and technology. These build on basic skills, thinking skills and personal qualities (US Department of Labor 1991, p. iii). The report emphasizes how globalization is changing the nature of work, for example, requiring capacities to work effectively with diverse groups and to understand systems.

Another ten years later, a coalition comprising the US Department of Education, one of the main teacher unions, and major technology companies, created an advocacy coalition, the Partnership for 21st Century Skills, to persuade states to broaden the goals of the curriculum which more explicitly focused on global content and cross-cultural skills.

Similar efforts to broaden the goals of the curriculum took place in other countries, as documented in a comparative study including Chile, China, India, Mexico, Singapore, and the United States (Reimers and Chung 2016). In addition, a number of international organizations advocated for intentional efforts to cultivate global competency. For example, in 2015 the World Economic Forum published a report identifying 16 key competencies for the twenty-first century, which included cultural literacy and social and cultural awareness (World Economic Forum 2015) and in a more recent report describing eight characteristics of high-quality learning for the fourth industrial revolution global citizenship skills top the list (World Economic Forum 2020a).

In response to the adoption of the United Nations Sustainable Development Goals by the UN General Assembly in September of 2015, UNESCO has advocated for the incorporation of cognitive and socio-emotional objectives into the curriculum aligned with those goals (UNESCO 2017a). One of the targets for Education SDG 4, on education, focuses specifically on global citizenship education, defined as follows:

> By 2030, ensure that all learners acquire the knowledge and skills needed to promote sustainable development, including, among others, through education for sustainable development and sustainable lifestyles, human rights, gender equality, promotion of a culture of peace and non-violence, global citizenship and appreciation of cultural diversity and of culture's contribution to sustainable development. (UN 2020)

The OECD has incorporated the assessment of global competency as part of the PISA program (OECD 2018). While PISA's measurement of skills is not related to existing curriculum, previous PISA studies have stimulated attention to standards and curriculum in various countries, and this new focus on global competence is likely to do the same. The OECD bases the assessment of global competence on this definition:

> Global competence is the capacity to examine local, global and intercultural issues, to understand and appreciate the perspectives and world views of others, to engage in open, appropriate and effective interactions with people from different cultures, and to act for collective well-being and sustainable development. (OECD 2018)

A working group convened by the UN, UNESCO, and the Brookings Institution to identify measurement instruments and approaches of global citizenship, synthesized their view of global competency in the following eight domains:

- Empathy
- Critical thinking and problem solving
- Ability to communicate and collaborate with others
- Conflict resolution
- Sense of security and identity
- Shared universal values (human rights, peace, justice)
- Respect for diversity and intercultural understanding
- Recognition of global issues and of their interconnectedness (Center for Universal Education 2017, p. 17).

A recent publication of the World Economic Forum defines Global Citizenship skills as:

> Include content that focuses on building awareness about the wider world, sustainability and playing an active role in the global community. (World Economic Forum 2020a, p. 4)

Animated by this new emphasis on making education relevant to a changing world, the last two decades have consequently seen remarkable transformation of public education systems around the world. Governments have focused more resources and attention on education, attempted more ambitious goals for education, and undertaken numerous innovations to achieve the audacious goal of preparing students for the twenty-first century. This enhanced education activity offers a rich reservoir of comparative experience about how governments approach the question of aligning public education systems with more ambitious goals. Learning from such comparative experience is the goal of the Global Education Innovation Initiative I lead at Harvard University. A collaborative with research institutions in several countries, we have carried out a series of studies to learn from such efforts to reform public education systems. We have studied national reform efforts to broaden the goals of the curriculum in Brazil, Chile, China, Colombia, Finland, Japan, Mexico, Poland, Portugal, Peru, Russia, Singapore, and the United States (Reimers and Chung 2016, 2018; Reimers 2020a, b).

These efforts to broaden national curriculum standards reflect increasing awareness of significant local and global challenges, as well as a commitment to bold aspirations to improve well-being and inclusion around the world.

3.3 Recent Imperatives for Global Education

Since 2006, the World Economic Forum produces an annual report on the major global risks. Drawing on the insights of a panel of experts and a survey of well-informed global leaders, the report identifies risks in terms of likelihood and impact. The risks identified are economic, environmental, geopolitical, societal, and technological. Economic risks include asset bubbles, deflation, failure of financial institutions, failure of critical infrastructure, fiscal crises, high structural unemployment or underemployment, illicit trade, severe energy price shock, and unmanageable inflation. Environmental risks include extreme weather, failure of climate change mitigation and adaptation, major biodiversity loss and ecosystem collapse, major natural disasters, and man-made environmental disasters. Geopolitical risks include failure of national governance, failure of regional or global governance, interstate conflict, large scale terrorist attacks, state collapse or crisis, and weapons of mass destruction. Societal risks include failure of urban planning, food crises, large-scale involuntary migration, profound social instability, rapid spread of infectious diseases, and water crises. Technological risks include adverse consequences of technological advances, critical information infrastructure breakdown, large-scale cyber-attacks, and massive data fraud and theft (World Economic Forum 2020b).

A recent report identifies as the most likely risks: extreme weather events, failure of climate change mitigation and adaptation, natural disasters, biodiversity loss, and man-made environmental disasters. In terms of potential impact, the top five risks are climate action failure, weapons of mass destruction, biodiversity loss, extreme weather events, and water crises (World Economic Forum 2020b).

It is noteworthy that many of the risks examined in the report, particularly those related to climate change, conflict and misuse of technology, have persisted as top risks for multiple years, underscoring that these are difficult issues to tackle, in part because they require global cooperation. This highlights three related motivations for global education. First, if we are to effectively manage those risks, people will need to be aware of them, care about them, and have the skills to address them. Helping people develop those understandings and skills is one goal of global education. Secondly, because these risks require difficult choices for governments, it is necessary that many people develop a deep understanding of these risks, so they can provide the political support necessary for governments to address them. Thirdly, as these risks require global cooperation it is necessary to help people in various countries gain these capacities, so governments can collaborate constructively with the support of their respective populations. All of this will be very difficult as illustrated by the 2019 World Economic Forum Global Risks Report which sounds an alarm bell on the complexity of the challenge of sustaining collective will to address these risks:

> Is the world sleepwalking into a crisis? Global risks are intensifying but the collective will to tackle them appears to be lacking. Instead, divisions are hardening. The world's move into a new phase of state-centered politics, noted in last year's Global Risks Report, continued throughout 2018…The energy now being expended on consolidating or recovering national control risks weakening collective responses to emerging global challenges. We are drifting

deeper into global problems from which we will struggle to extricate ourselves. (World Economic Forum 2019)

One of the most severe global risks, climate catastrophe, has dominated the risk assessment for several years. The Intergovernmental Panel on Climate Change has stated that we have a decade to put in place serious changes to prevent global temperatures from rising above 1.5 °C (IPCC 2018). In the United States, the National Climate Assessment warned that absent significant reductions in emissions, average global temperatures could rise by 5 °C by the end of the century (National Climate Assessment 2018). These changes in climate will have a number of negative effects. A recent UN report predicts global disruptions in the supply of food, and food shortages will likely cause involuntary cross-national migrations. To prevent further climate change, the report calls for changes in food consumption and agriculture production (IPCC 2018). A recent report documents that 17 nations are currently experiencing extreme water stress, which could impact a quarter of the world's population (Hofste et al. 2019). These changes will in turn induce other changes that will impact sustainability. For instance, warming oceans are leading to an increase in methylmecury, a neurotoxicant, in fish. The increased levels of methylmercury in fish will impact marine life and humans who consume fish (Schartup et al. 2019).

These global trends and risks interact with each other, potentially compounding their effects. For example, in the United States, there are partisan political divides in how much confidence people have in scientists, which limits the credibility of scientists to inform public understanding on some of the critical global risks, such as climate change. Whereas 43% of Democrats report that they have a great deal of confidence in scientists to act in the best interest of the public, only 27% of Republicans share this view. Confidence in scientists increases with the level of science knowledge of the person, for those with low levels of science knowledge, only 26% report a great deal of confidence in scientists, compared to 45% among those with high levels of science knowledge who report a great deal of confidence in scientists (Funk et al. 2019, p. 3).

A particular challenge to global education is the emergence of new forms of tribalism, variations of intolerant and xenophobic nationalism, which explicitly challenge democratic norms and cosmopolitan ideas. A significant percentage of the world's population is dissatisfied with how democracy works in their country: 51% on average in 27 countries (Wike et al. 2019). Dissatisfaction with democracy is related to economic frustration, the status of individual rights and the belief that political elites are disconnected from the concerns of ordinary citizens and are corrupt (Ibid).

Societies are divided over race, religion, class and how they view immigrants, one of the manifestations of globalization. Over the last decade, government restrictions and social hostilities based on religion have increased in 52 countries surveyed by the Pew Organization (Pew Research Center 2019). In the United States, the FBI has reported an increase in hate crimes over three consecutive years, with a 22% increase in 2017, more than half of which were anti-Semitic incidents (Byrd 2018).

Demographic changes and immigration are changing the ethnic and racial composition of many societies. This augments the urgency of educating people to understand the positive potential of diversity and to equip them to work productively and to be able to find common ground across differences. In a more diverse context, the severe harm and conflict that prejudice and bigotry begets can augment its impact. In the United States, for example, higher population growth for minority groups and declining birth rates among whites will result in a country where ethnic minority groups will constitute the majority of the population by 2045. Whites will account for 49.7% of the population, Hispanics for 24.6%, blacks 13.1%, Asians 7.9%, and multiracial groups 3.8% (Frey 2018). "Most Americans (57%) say the fact that the U.S. population is made up of people of many different races and ethnicities is a very good thing for the country, and another 20% say this is somewhat good. Smaller shares say this is somewhat (5%) or very (1%) bad, while 17% say it is neither good nor bad for the country. Similar shares of whites (55%), blacks (59%) and Hispanics (60%) say racial and ethnic diversity is very good for the country" (Horowitz 2019).

In spite of these positive views held by the majority of the population about racial and ethnic diversity, a recent survey administered to a nationally representative sample of Americans on attitudes toward race in the United States shows that the majority of the population (58%) believes that race relations are generally bad. This percentage is higher among blacks (71%) than whites (56%) as shown in Fig. 3.1 (Horowitz et al. 2019).

> Most Americans (65%) – including majorities across racial and ethnic groups – say it has become more common for people to express racist or racially insensitive views since Trump was elected president. A smaller but substantial share (45%) say this has become more acceptable. (Horowitz et al. 2019)

> About three-quarters of blacks and Asians (76% of each) – and 58% of Hispanics – say they have experienced discrimination or have been treated unfairly because of their race or ethnicity at least from time to time. In contrast, about two-thirds of whites (67%) say they've never experienced this. (Ibid)

Public opinion surveys also document discrimination against immigrants globally. While the majority see immigrants as a strength, there are also many who see them as a burden to the country. Figure 3.2 summarizes the results of a 2018 Pew Research Survey in 18 countries, which account for half of the world's population of migrants, in which people were asked whether immigrants made the country stronger or whether they were a burden.

Liberal democracies are experiencing a number of challenges reflected in declining support for democracy and decline in democracy around the world. In 2018 democratic freedoms declined in 71 countries, whereas they improved in only 35 countries—the twelfth consecutive year of decline of democracy globally (Abramowitz 2018). A survey conducted by the Pew Research Center in 38 nations shows that while representative democracy is preferred by the majority of the population, there is also significant support for non-democratic ways of government. Just under half of the population across these countries favors a system in which experts make decisions instead of elected representatives, and one in four persons thinks a

Fig. 3.1 Views of racial progress in the United States, among blacks and whites. *Source* Horowitz et al. (2019)

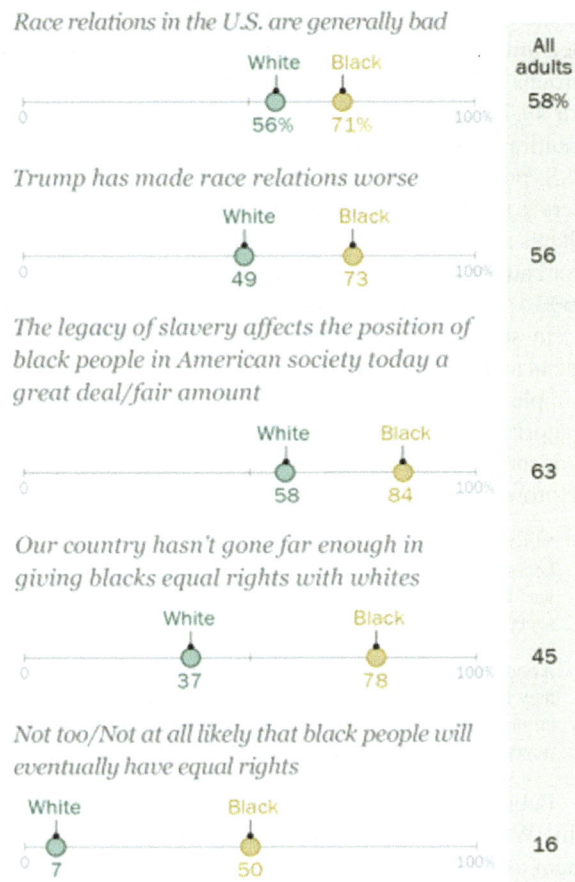

Fig. 3.2 How do people see immigrants. *Source* Gonzalez-Barrera and Connor (2019)

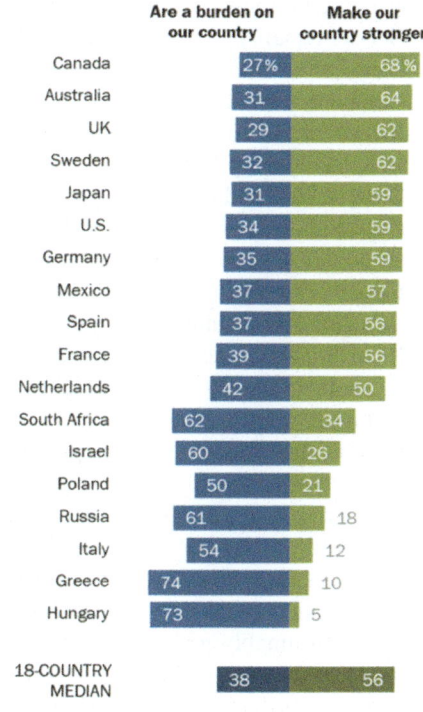

system in which a strong leader can make decisions without interference from parliament or the courts would be a very good way to govern (Wike and Fetterolf 2018, p. 139). Another 24% believe that a system ruled by the military would be very good (Ibid).

Against the backdrop of these global risks and challenges, a hopeful vision for the future of the world is expressed in a compact of seventeen goals, adopted at the UN General Assembly in September of 2015, which articulate the conditions for a world which is inclusive and sustainable. These goals are:

1. No poverty: End Poverty in all its forms everywhere.
2. Zero hunger: End hunger, achieve food security and improved nutrition and promote sustainable agriculture.
3. Good health and well-being: Ensure healthy lives and promote well-being for all at all ages.
4. Quality education: Ensure inclusive and equitable quality education and promote lifelong learning opportunities for all.
5. Gender equality: Achieve gender equality and empower all women and girls.
6. Clean water and sanitation: Ensure availability and sustainable management of water and sanitation for all.
7. Affordable and clean energy: Ensure access to affordable, reliable, sustainable and clean energy for all.
8. Decent work and economic growth: Promote sustained, inclusive and sustainable economic growth, full and productive employment and decent work for all.
9. Industry, innovation, and infrastructure: Build resilient infrastructure, promote inclusive and sustainable industrialization and foster innovation.
10. Reduce inequalities: Reduce inequality within and among countries.
11. Sustainable cities and communities: Make cities and human settlements inclusive, safe, resilient, and sustainable.
12. Responsible consumption and production: Ensure sustainable consumption and production patterns.
13. Climate action: Take urgent steps to combat climate change and its impacts.
14. Life below water: Conserve and sustainably use the oceans, seas, and marine resources for sustainable development.
15. Life on land: Protect, restore, and promote sustainable use of terrestrial ecosystems, sustainably manage forests, combat desertification, and halt and reverse land degradation, and halt biodiversity loss.
16. Peace, justice and strong institutions: Promote peaceful and inclusive societies for sustainable development, provide access to justice for all and build effective, accountable, and inclusive institutions at all levels.
17. Partnership for the goals: Strengthen the means of implementation and revitalize the global partnership for sustainable development (UN 2020).

Each of these goals has in turn a number of specific targets, which operationalize the goals. As mentioned earlier, goal number 4, for example, focused on quality education for all, includes a target which focuses on global citizenship education, in ways reminiscent of the language of the right to education in the Universal Declaration of Human Rights, reflecting cosmopolitan views of the enlightenment:

> Target 4.7: By 2030 ensure all learners acquire knowledge and skills needed to promote sustainable development, including among others through education for sustainable development and sustainable lifestyles, human rights, gender equality, promotion of a culture of peace and non-violence, global citizenship, and appreciation of cultural diversity and of culture's contribution to sustainable development. (UN 2020)

3.3 Recent Imperatives for Global Education

An intentional global education which responds to these cultural imperatives would create opportunities for students to learn about and develop the skills to address the kinds of risks identified by the World Economic Forum and to contribute to achieving the United Nations Development Goals. These broad and ambitious development goals can inform the development of curriculum.

In 2009–2010, with a group of my graduate students, I developed a comprehensive curriculum, spanning from kindergarten to high school, aligned with the UN SDGs (we initially worked with the Millennium Development Goals, and later on substituted them with the Sustainable Development Goals as they were adopted at the UN General Assembly in 2015), with the Universal Declaration of Human Rights, and with the World Economic Forum Risk Assessment Framework. From the study of those goals, we developed a framework of competencies which a high school graduate should have in order to contribute to achieving such goals. Then, we used this framework to guide the development of 350 units to be taught in a special course, a "world course," that would provide students explicit opportunities to integrate knowledge gained in various disciplines, as they worked on projects aligned with those competencies (Reimers et al. 2016).

"… the overarching goal of our curriculum is to support the development of global citizenship, which is understood to be the result of competencies in understanding, caring about, and having the capacity to influence global affairs and to advance human rights. We built on a conceptualization of global competency that included knowledge, affect, and skills (Reimers 2009, 2010). Central to our conception of global competency is the notion of human agency—of empowerment—and we therefore sought to cultivate the mindset that individuals can make a difference, the desire to take initiative, the ability to act in leadership roles, and an understanding of responsibility.

The principles that guided our curriculum design were: defining clear outcomes for knowledge, affect, and action and focusing on interdisciplinary units that would be aligned with coherent themes in each grade, as well as with an overall scope and sequence. Finally, we audited the entire curriculum to ascertain whether there were adequate opportunities for developing the intended capabilities throughout. We balanced the curriculum mapping with various features designed to support personalization, such as providing students with opportunities to develop their own interests, discover their passions, and learn deeply about issues that were of interest to them. In particular, we relied on project-based learning, student collaboration, engagement from parents and community members, and student agency in shaping the high school curriculum as ways to personalize learning.

One of the pedagogical principles on which this design was grounded was to rely extensively on project-based learning and on active learning methodologies, such as Design Thinking, that place students at the center of their learning. We also sought to give students abundant opportunities to demonstrate understanding in the form of products that could be shared with peers, teachers, and other audiences, including students in other grades in the school and parents.

We also created multiple opportunities for students to directly collaborate with peers in other countries with the use of technology for project-based work and remote communication. We viewed this collaboration as a way to help them discover their common humanity with diverse students.

The curriculum also provides multiple opportunities to directly engage students and teachers with parents and community members who can directly contribute knowledge and experience to support global education, and thereby help students identify authentic connections between the local and global.

Throughout the entire K-12 curriculum, but particularly in grades nine through twelve, are opportunities for students to pursue their personal interests with greater depth, and to co-construct with their teachers a significant portion of the curriculum.

We defined those competencies as encompassing intercultural competency, ethical orientation, knowledge and skills, and work and mind habits:

1. **Intercultural competency**

   This includes the ability to interact successfully with people from different cultural identities and origins. It encompasses interpersonal skills as well as intrapersonal skills and ways to govern oneself in the face of cultural differences.

   A. Interpersonal Skills
      i. Work productively in and effectively lead intercultural teams, including teams distributed in various geographies through the use of telecommunication technologies
      ii. Demonstrate empathy toward other people from different cultural origins
      iii. Demonstrate courtesy and norms of interaction appropriate to various cultural settings
      iv. Resolve culturally based disagreements through negotiation, mediation, and conflict resolution
   B. Intrapersonal Skills
      i. Curiosity about global affairs and world cultures
      ii. The ability to recognize and weigh diverse cultural perspectives
      iii. An understanding of one's own identity, of others' identities, of how other cultures shape their own and others' identities, and of where one is in space and time
      iv. The ability to recognize and examine assumptions when engaging with cultural differences
      v. The recognition of cultural (civilizational, religious, or ethnic) prejudice and the ability to minimize its effects in intergroup dynamics
      vi. An understanding and appreciation of cultural variation in basic norms of interaction, the ability to be courteous, and the ability to find and learn about norms appropriate in specific settings and types of interaction

2. **Ethical orientation**

   A. Appreciation of ethical frameworks in diverse religious systems
   B. Commitment to basic equality of all people
   C. Recognition of common values and common humanity across civilizational streams

3.3 Recent Imperatives for Global Education

    D. Appreciation of the potential of every person regardless of socioeconomic circumstances or cultural origin
    E. Appreciation of the role of global compacts such as the Universal Declaration of Human Rights in guiding global governance
    F. Commitment to supporting universal human rights, to reducing global poverty, to promoting peace, and to promoting sustainable forms of human–environmental interaction
    G. Ability to interact with people from diverse cultural backgrounds while demonstrating humility, respect, reciprocity, and integrity
    H. An understanding of the role of trust in sustaining human interaction as well as global institutions and recognition of forms of breakdowns in trust and institutional corruption and its causes

3. **Knowledge and skills**
In addition to highlighting the cosmopolitan links infused in the curriculum, as Kandel recommended a century ago, a global education curriculum should provide students with the knowledge and skills necessary to understand the various vectors of globalization. These include culture, religion, history and geography, politics and government, economics, science, technology and innovation, public health, and demography.

    A. Culture, religion, and history and geography
        i. World history and geography, with attention to the role of globalization in cultural change
        ii. The study of religions as powerful institutions organizing human activity
        iii. Historical knowledge, which includes various perspectives and an understanding of the role of ordinary citizens in history
        iv. World geography, including the different areas of the world, what unites them, what differences exist, and how humans have changed the geography of the planet
        v. World religions, history, and points of contact between civilizations over time
        vi. Major philosophical traditions and points of connection
        vii. Performing and visual arts (e.g., theater, dance, music, visual arts, etc.) as a means to find common humanity
        viii. Different arts and ability to see connections
        ix. Ability to view art as expression, to use art for expression, and to understand globalization and art
    B. Politics and government
        i. Comparative government
        ii. How governments work in different societies
        iii. Major international institutions and their role in shaping global affairs
        iv. Contemporary global challenges in human–environmental interaction

       v. Sources of these challenges, options to address them, and the role of global institutions in addressing these challenges
      vi. History of contemporary global conflicts and the role of global institutions in addressing these challenges
- C. Economics, business, and entrepreneurship
  - i. Theories of economic development and how they explain the various stages in economic development of nations, poverty, and inequality
  - ii. Institutions that regulate global trade and work to promote international development
  - iii. Contemporary literature on the effectiveness and limitations of those institutions
  - iv. The impact of global trade
  - v. The consequences of global poverty and the agency of the poor
  - vi. The demography and factors influencing demographic trends and their implications for global change
- D. Science, technology and innovation, and globalization
- E. Public Health, population, and demography

4. Work and mind habits

- A. Demonstrate innovation and creativity in contributing to formulating solutions to global challenges and to seizing global opportunities; seek and identify the best global practices; and transfer them across geographic, disciplinary, and professional contexts
- B. Identify different cultural perspectives through which to think about problems
- C. Understand the process of cultural change and that there is individual variation within cultural groups
- D. Carry out research projects independently
- E. Present results of independent research in writing, orally, and using media." (Reimers et al. 2016, pp. lvii–lx).

In 2016, working with 36 of my graduate students, we developed a streamlined global education curriculum, from kindergarten to high school, following the same process of backward design from the UN Sustainable Development Goals (Reimers et al. 2017). A year later, with another group of 34 graduate students, we developed a variety of different curriculum prototypes, also aligned with the UN Sustainable Development Goals (Reimers et al. 2018).

UNESCO also developed a series of learning objectives aligned to the UN Sustainable Development Goals, which can be used to develop programs, curriculum or instructional materials in any country. Cross-cutting competencies for sustainability identified in the report include systems thinking, anticipatory competency, normative competency, strategic competency, collaboration competency, critical thinking competency, self-awareness and integrated problem-solving competency (UNESCO

3.3 Recent Imperatives for Global Education

2017a, p. 10). Specific learning objectives aligned with each SDG include cognitive, socio-emotional and behavioral objectives. For example, with respect to the first SDG: No Poverty, the UNESCO report identifies the following objectives:

Cognitive learning objectives

1. The learner understands the concepts of extreme and relative poverty and is able to critically reflect on their underlying cultural and normative assumptions and practices.
2. The learner knows about the local, national and global distribution of extreme poverty and extreme wealth.
3. The learner knows about causes and impacts of poverty such as unequal distribution of resources and power, colonization, conflicts, disasters caused by natural hazards and other climate change-induced impacts, environmental degradation and technological disasters, and the lack of social protection systems and measures.
4. The learner understands how extremes of poverty and extremes of wealth affect basic human rights and needs.
5. The learner knows about poverty reduction strategies and measures and is able to distinguish between deficit-based and strength-based approaches to addressing poverty.

Socio-emotional learning objectives

1. The learner is able to collaborate with others to empower individuals and communities to affect change in the distribution of power and resources in the community and beyond.
2. The learner is able to raise awareness about extremes of poverty and wealth and encourage dialogue about solutions.
3. The learner is able to show sensitivity to the issues of poverty as well as empathy and solidarity with poor people and those in vulnerable situations.
4. The learner is able to identify their personal experiences and biases with respect to poverty.
5. The learner is able to reflect critically on their own role maintaining global structures of inequality.

Behavioral learning objectives

1. The learner is able to plan, implement, evaluate and replicate activities that contribute to poverty reduction.
2. The learner is able to publicly demand and support the development and integration of politics that promote social and economic justice, risk reduction strategies and poverty eradication actions.
3. The learner is able to evaluate, participate in and influence decision-making related to management strategies of local, national and international enterprises concerning poverty generation and eradication.
4. The learner is able to include poverty reduction, social justice and anti-corruption considerations in their consumption activities.
5. The learner is able to propose solutions to address systemic-problems related to poverty. (UNESCO 2017a, p. 12)

References

Abramowitz, M. (2018). *Freedom in the world 2018: Democracy in crisis.* Freedom House. https://freedomhouse.org/article/democracy-crisis-freedom-house-releases-freedom-world-2018.

Adams, J. Q. (1804). *Letters on Silesia. Written during a tour through that country during the years 1800, 1801.* London: Printed for J. Budd at the Crown and Mitre Pall Mall. https://archive.org/details/lettersonsilesi00adamgoog/page/n383.

Byrd, D. (2018). *FBI report: Religion-based hate crimes in 2017 increased for the third consecutive year.* https://bjconline.org/fbi-report-religion-based-hate-crimes-up-22-in-2017-111318/.

Center for Universal Education at Brookings. (2017). *Measuring global citizenship education. A collection of practices and tools.* Washington, DC: Brookings Institution. https://www.brookings.edu/wp-content/uploads/2017/04/global_20170411_measuring-global-citizenship.pdf.

Davies, I., Ho, L. C., Kiwan, D., Peck, C. L., Peterson, A., Sant, E., et al. (Eds.). (2018). *The Palgrave handbook of global citizenship and education.* London, UK: Palgrave Macmillan.

Delors, J. (1996). *Learning: The treasure within, report to UNESCO of the international commission on education for the twenty-first century.* Paris: UNESCO.

Faure, E., Herrera, F., Kaddoura, A. R., Lopes, H., Petrovsky, A., Rahnema, M., et al. (1972). *Learning to be: The world of education today and tomorrow.* Paris: UNESCO.

Frey, W. (2018, March 14). *The US will become "minority white" in 2045, census projects.* https://www.brookings.edu/blog/the-avenue/2018/03/14/the-us-will-become-minority-white-in-2045-census-projects/.

Funk, C., Hefferon, M., Kennedy, B., & Johnson, C. (2019, August 2). *Trust and mistrust in American's views of scientific experts.* Pew Research Organization.

Gonzalez-Barrera, A., & Connor, P. (2019). *Around the world, more say immigrants are a strength than a burden.* Pew Research Organization. https://www.pewresearch.org/global/2019/03/14/around-the-world-more-say-immigrants-are-a-strength-than-a-burden/.

Hofste, R., Reig, P., & Schleifer, L. (2019). *17 countries, home to one-quarter of the world's population, face extremely high water stress.* https://www.wri.org/blog/2019/08/17-countries-home-one-quarter-world-population-face-extremely-high-water-stress.

Horowitz, J. M. (2019). *Americans see advantages and challenges in country's growing racial and ethnic diversity.* https://www.pewsocialtrends.org/2019/05/08/americans-see-advantages-and-challenges-in-countrys-growing-racial-and-ethnic-diversity/.

Horowitz, J. M., Brown, A., & Cox, K. (2019). *Race in America 2019.* https://www.pewsocialtrends.org/2019/04/09/race-in-america-2019/.

IPCC (2018) *Summary for policymakers. In: Global Warming of 1.5°C. An IPCC Special Report on the impacts of global warming of 1.5°C above pre-industrial levels and related global greenhouse gas emission pathways, in the context of strengthening the global response to the threat of climate change, sustainable development, and efforts to eradicate poverty* [Masson-Delmotte, V., P. Zhai, H.-O. Pörtner, D. Roberts, J. Skea, P.R. Shukla, A. Pirani, W. Moufouma-Okia, C. Péan, R. Pidcock, S. Connors, J.B.R. Matthews, Y. Chen, X. Zhou, M.I. Gomis, E. Lonnoy, T. Maycock, M. Tignor, and T. Waterfield (eds.)]. In Press. https://www.ipcc.ch/site/assets/uploads/sites/2/2019/05/SR15_SPM_version_report_LR.pdf.

Jullien, M. A. (1812). *Esprit de la méthode d'éducation de Pestalozzi, suivie et pratiquée dans l'Institut d'Éducation d'Yverdun, en Suisse.* Milan: De L'imprimerie royale. https://archive.org/details/espritdelamthod00jullgoog/page/n6.

Jullien, M. A. (1817a). *Esquisse et vues préliminaires d'un ouvrage sur l'éducation comparée, et séries de questions sur l'éducation.* Paris: I. Colas.

Jullien, M. A. (1817b, November 30). Letter of Marc Antoine Jullien to Thomas Jeffferson. https://founders.archives.gov/documents/Jefferson/03-12-02-0181.

Jullien, M. A. (1835). *Essai général d'éducation physique, morale et intellectuelle. Suivi d'un plan d'éducation pratique pour l'enfance, l'adolescence et la jeunesse, ou recherches sur les principes d'une éducation perfectionnée.* Paris. https://archive.org/stream/essaignraldeduca00jull/essaignraldeduca00jull_djvu.txt.

References

Jullien, M. A. (1842). *Exposé de la méthode d'éducation de Pestalozzi, telle qu'elle a été pratiquée sous sa direction pendant dix années de 1806 à 1816 dans l'institut d'Yverdun, en Suisse.* Paris: L. Hachette. Libraire de L'Universite. https://archive.org/details/exposedelamtho00jull/page/n14.

Kant, I. (1795). *Perpetual peace: A philosophical sketch.* Philadelphia, PA: Slougth Foundation and Syracuse University Humanities Center. https://slought.org/media/files/perpetual_peace.pdf.

Mann, H. (1844). *Remarks on the seventh annual report of the Hon. Horace Mann.* Boston: Charles Little and James Brown. https://babel.hathitrust.org/cgi/pt?id=mdp.39015003458208&view=1up&seq=7.

NAFSA. (2003). Securing America's future: Global education for a global age report of the strategic task force on education abroad. Retrieved January 23, 2020, from https://www.nafsa.org/sites/default/files/ektron/uploadedFiles/NAFSA_Home/Resource_Library_Assets/Public_Policy/securing_america_s_future.pdf.

National Climate Assessment. (2018). *Fourth national climate assesment.* https://nca2018.globalchange.gov/.

OECD. (2018). *PISA 2018 results.* https://www.oecd.org/pisa/publications/pisa-2018-results.htm.

Pew Research Center. (2019). *A closer look at how religious restrictions have risen around the world.* https://www.pewforum.org/2019/07/15/a-closer-look-at-how-religious-restrictions-have-risen-around-the-world/.

Piaget, J. (1993). Jan Amos Comenius. *Prospects, XXIII*(1/2), 173–196. http://www.ibe.unesco.org/sites/default/files/comeniuse.PDF (UNESCO, International Bureau of Education).

Reimers, F., Chopra, V., Chung, C., Higdon, J., & O'Donnell, E. B. (2016). *Empowering global citizens.* Charleston, SC: CreateSpace.

Reimers, F., & Chung, C. (Eds.). (2016). *Teaching and learning for the twenty first century.* Cambridge: Harvard Education Press.

Reimers, F., et al. (2017). *Empowering students to improve the world in sixty lessons.* Charleston, SC: CreateSpace.

Reimers, F., et al. (2018). *Learning to collaborate for the global common good.* Charleston, SC: CreateSpace.

Reimers, F., & Chung, C. (Eds.). (2018). *Preparing teachers to educate whole students: An international comparative study.* Cambridge, MA: Harvard Education Publishing.

Reimers, F. (2020a). *Audacious education purposes.* Springer (in press).

Reimers, F. (2020b). *Empowering teachers to build a better world.* Springer (in press).

Roser, M., & Ortiz-Ospina, E. (2019). *Primary and secondary education.* https://ourworldindata.org/primary-and-secondary-education#the-rise-of-basic-schooling-over-the-last-2-centuries.

Rychen, D. (2003). Key competencies: Meeting important challenges in life. In Rychen, D. S. & Salganik, L. H. *Key competencies for a successful life and a well-functioning society* (pp. 63–107). Seattle: Hogrefe and Huber Publishers.

Rychen, D. S., & Salganik, L. H. (2001). *Defining and selecting key competencies.* Seattle: Hogrefe and Huber Publishers.

Rychen, D. S., & Salganik, L. H. (2003). *Key competencies for a successful life and a well-functioning society.* Seattle: Hogrefe and Huber Publishers.

Sarmiento, D. F. (1849). *De la Educacion Popular.* Santiago: Imprenta de Julio Belin y Compania.

Schartup, A., Thackray, C., Qureshi, A., Dassuncao, C., Gillespie, K., Hanke, A., & Sunderland, E. (2019). Climate change and overfishing increase neurotoxicant in marine predators. *Nature.* Published: 7 August 2019.

Soetard, M. (1994a) Jean-Jaques Rousseau (1712–78). In *Prospects: quarterly review of comparative education* (Vol. XXIV, No. 3/4, pp. 423–438). Paris, UNESCO: International Bureau of Education.

Soetard, M. (1994b). Johann Heinrich Pestalozzi (1746–1827). In *Prospects: The quarterly review of comparative education* (Vol. XXIV, No. 1/2, pp. 297–310). Paris, UNESCO: International Bureau of Education.

United Nations. (1948). *Universal declaration of human rights.* https://www.un.org/en/universal-declaration-human-rights/.

United States Department of Labor. (1991). *What work requires of schools. A Scans report for America.* https://wdr.doleta.gov/SCANS/whatwork/whatwork.pdf.

United States National Commission on Excellence in Education. (1983). *A nation at risk: The imperative for educational reform a report to the nation and the secretary of education.* United States Department of Education. https://www2.ed.gov/pubs/NatAtRisk/index.html.

UNESCO (1974) *Recommendation concerning education for international understanding, co-operation and peace and education relating to human rights and fundamental freedoms.* http://portal.unesco.org/en/ev.php-URL_ID=13088&URL_DO=DO_TOPIC&URL_SECTION=201.html.

UNESCO. (2017). *Education for sustainable development goals learning objectives.* Paris: UNESCO.

United Nations. (2020). Sustainable development goals. Retrieved January 23, 2020, from https://www.un.org/sustainabledevelopment/education/.

Wike, R., & Fetterolf, J. (2018). Liberal democracy's crisis of confidence. *Journal of Democracy, 29*(4), 136–150.

Wike, R., Silver, L., & Castillo, A. (2019). *Many across the globe are dissatisfied with how democracy is working.* Pew Research Organization. Retrieved April 29, 2019.

World Economic Forum. (2015). *New vision for education. Unlocking the potential of technology.* http://www3.weforum.org/docs/WEFUSA_NewVisionforEducation_Report2015.pdf.

World Economic Forum. (2019). The global risks report. Retrieved January 23, 2020, from https://www.weforum.org/reports/the-global-risks-report-2019.

World Economic Forum. (2020a). Schools of the future. Defining new models of education for the fourth industrial revolution.

World Economic Forum. (2020b). The global risks report. Retrieved January 23, 2020, from https://www.weforum.org/reports/the-global-risks-report-2020.

Open Access This chapter is licensed under the terms of the Creative Commons Attribution 4.0 International License (http://creativecommons.org/licenses/by/4.0/), which permits use, sharing, adaptation, distribution and reproduction in any medium or format, as long as you give appropriate credit to the original author(s) and the source, provide a link to the Creative Commons license and indicate if changes were made.

The images or other third party material in this chapter are included in the chapter's Creative Commons license, unless indicated otherwise in a credit line to the material. If material is not included in the chapter's Creative Commons license and your intended use is not permitted by statutory regulation or exceeds the permitted use, you will need to obtain permission directly from the copyright holder.

Chapter 4
A Psychological Perspective and Global Education

The knowledge generated by the science of how people learn and develop can inform the design of global education curricula and instruction. A synthesis of the evidence on twenty-first-century skills prepared by an expert group convened by the National Research Council in the United States grouped those skills, building on Bloom's taxonomy, in three broad domains of competence: cognitive, intrapersonal, and interpersonal. Cognitive competencies include cognitive processing and strategies, knowledge and creativity; intrapersonal competencies include intellectual openness, work ethic, and conscientiousness; interpersonal competencies include teamwork, collaboration, and leadership (Pellegrino and Hilton 2012). The review shows that there is a larger and more robust body of scientific evidence supporting the importance of cognitive competencies for long term outcomes than for the inter- and intrapersonal competencies. Among intra- and interpersonal competencies, conscientiousness (organization, responsibility, and hard work) are most clearly related to positive educational, career and health outcomes, whereas antisocial behavior is most clearly negatively associated with those outcomes (Pellegrino and Hilton 2012, pp. 4–5). The report also examined "deeper learning" the process that allows a person to transfer what was learned and apply it to a new situation. This includes "content knowledge in a domain and knowledge of how, why, and when to apply this knowledge to answer questions and solve problems" which the report calls twenty-first-century competencies (Ibid, p. 6). Cultivating the full range of twenty-first-century competencies requires additional instructional time and resources than is common and supports the idea of engaging students in projects of longer duration, spanning several weeks, even months.

This report shows how an integrated science curriculum can promote deeper learning in which students gain content knowledge as well as intrapersonal and interpersonal competencies, this is illustrative of the kind of curriculum which could promote deep global competence, this curriculum "combined collaborative, hands-on science inquiry activities with reading text, writing notes and reports, and small group discussions…students exposed to the integrated curriculum demonstrated significantly greater gains on measures of science understanding, science vocabulary, and science writing. At the same time, the students developed the intrapersonal competencies of oral communication and discourse, as well as the interpersonal competencies of metacognition and positive dispositions towards learning." (Ibid, p. 7). The report draws out recommendations for curriculum and instructional design which reflect the principles uncovered by the science of deeper learning as helpful to developing twenty-first-century skills. They include establishing clear learning goals and a model of how learning develops, coupled with assessment to measure progress toward the goals, beginning in the earliest grades and sustained throughout their careers. The recommendations include also using multiple representations of concepts and tasks, encouraging elaboration, questioning, and explanation, engaging learners in challenging tasks, teaching with examples and cases, activating students' motivation by connecting topics to students' personal experience, and using formative assessment.

The design of the World Course, described earlier, was based on many of those same principles, particularly clear learning goals, integrating cognitive goals with intra- and interpersonal goals, organized in a coherent curricular sequence starting earlier, and with multiple representations of concepts to engage learners in challenging tasks and connecting new content with personal and immediate experiences of learners. Notice how this differs from "sprinkling" a few lessons related to global goals, such as the UN SDGs here and there, without a clear sequence or explicit articulation with the rest of the academic curriculum.

An effective global education curriculum needs good and rigorous design that effectively relates to content as well as to the cross-cutting twenty-first-century skills. For example, the first unit of the World Course in the second grade covers similarities and differences across cultures. The unit covers various related themes: (a) knowledge: diverse cultural perspectives, variations within groups, geography, common values, use of evidence, use of technology; (b) intrapersonal: curiosity about global affairs, and (c) interpersonal: empathy. This unit is to be developed in six activities and twelve lessons over an eight-week period, in this way permitting sustained engagement over an extended period, and permitting students to understand deeply the structure of the concepts taught, to have multiple opportunities to demonstrate understanding and receive feedback. The unit spells out goals and objectives, skills and knowledge, and six activities:

The World Course

Unit   2.1

Topic   **Similarities and Differences Across Cultures**

Theme   **Diverse cultural perspectives, empathy, variations within cultural groups, curiosity about global affairs, geography, common values, the use of evidence, and the use of technology**

Region   **Any/all, with more emphasis on the countries represented by the children's parents and on the countries in which partner schools are located. It would be helpful if various sections of the same grade covered different countries and attempted to have a representation of various world regions (e.g., Africa, Asia, Europe, and Latin America)**

Length   **Eight weeks (six activities and twelve sessions)**

Goals and Objectives

1. **Learn** similarities and differences in how children play in different cultures and understand the limitations of representing an entire culture or country with ideal types or averages, understanding that within every culture, there is variation.
2. **Inspire** students to take interest in various cultures, cultural differences, and the ways children live in different cultures. Spark their desire to communicate with children in other countries with the use of modern telecommunication technologies.
3. **Act** by describing the games children play in different cultures and sharing those observations with students in other parts of the world.

Skills and Knowledge

1. Students will describe the games that they and other children in their school play and then present those descriptions in a poster.
2. Students will analyze and compare various games played by children in their school.
3. Students will narrate the games they play, produce simple videos and pictures of those games, and share those observations with peers in other countries using Internet-based communication technologies
4. Students will analyze reports produced by peers in a school in another country describing the games they play.

Overview

This unit engages students in the analysis of their direct experience with the games they play, and that analysis is then extended to analyses of the games played by their parents and their peers in other countries. The activities involve collecting evidence, using observation skills, studying interviews and documentary sources, elaborating a framework creating categories to analyze games, and presenting analyses to peers and teachers in their school and to peers in other countries. The unit offers an introduction to maps and to countries and students around the world. Students use technology to communicate with peers in other countries.

Activity 2.1.2 What Games Did Our Parents Play When They Were Children?

Activity 2.1.3 Observing Children Play

Activity 2.1.4 Talking about Games with Children in Other Parts of the World

Activity 2.1.5 Understanding Maps

Activity 2.1.6 Learning about Games in Other Countries (Reimers et al. 2016, pp. 54–61).

The same format was followed in designing each of the 350 units comprising the World Course curriculum, all of them sequenced in a progression designed to develop the various cognitive, intra- and interdisciplinary competencies described earlier. The units in each grade were structured in a coherent scope and sequence that engaged students in a year-long project, leading up to a capstone product that demonstrates their understanding. The capstones are: kindergarteners take part in a puppet show performance on understanding difference, first graders create a "Book of Me," second graders educate others, third graders create a business (chocolate), fourth graders create a game about civilizations, fifth graders create an awareness project on SDGs, sixth graders implement an advocacy project about an SDG, seventh graders participate in extended service-learning, and eighth graders create a social enterprise around an SDG. In many cases, the capstone activities build on one another; in fifth grade, for example, students are asked to create an awareness project to inform others about the SDGs, and in sixth grade, they are then asked to implement an advocacy project about the SDGs.

In the World Course, there is also coherence across grades, each of which focuses on one particular theme as seen below.

The World Course: Kindergarten through Eighth Grade

Kindergarten	*Our World Is Diverse and Beautiful*
First Grade	*We Are One People with Universal Human Needs*
Second Grade	*Ourselves and Others*
Third Grade	*Understanding Global Interdependence through Entrepreneurship in Chocolate Manufacturing*
Fourth Grade	*The Rise (and Fall) of Ancient and Modern Civilizations*
Fifth Grade	*Freedom and the Rights of Individuals: Social Change around the Rights of Individuals*
Sixth Grade	*How Values and Identities Shape People and Institutions*
Seventh Grade	*Driving Change in Society by Organizing as a Collective and through the Study of Change Makers*
Eight Grade	*Migration*

The World Course: Ninth through Twelfth Grade

High School Semester Course	*The Environment*
High School Semester Course	*Society and Public Health Course*
High School Semester Course	*Global Conflicts and Resolutions*
High School Semester Course	*Development Economics: Growth and Development in Latin America*
High School Semester Course	*Technology, Innovation, and Globalization* (Reimers et al. 2016)

These capstones and thematic foci per grade provide students opportunities to work for an extended time on a problem or problem space, in ways which research suggests are productive to develop twenty-first-century skills. The Synthesis by Pellegrino and Hilton, drawing on two meta-analyses of research on project-based learning identifies six key principles of problem-based learning:

> PBL approaches represent learning tasks in the form of rich extended problems that, if carefully designed and implemented, can engage learnings in challenging tasks (problems) while providing guidance and feedback. They can encourage elaboration, questioning, and self-explanation and can prime motivation by presenting problems that are relevant and interesting to the learners. While a variety of different approaches to PBL have been developed, such instruction often follows six key principles:
>
> 1. Student-centered learning
> 2. Small groups
> 3. Tutor as a facilitator or guide

4. Problems first
5. The problem is the tool to achieve knowledge and problem-solving skills
6. Self-directed learning (Pellegrino and Hilton 2012, p. 166).

Here are additional instructional implications for global education drawn from a recent synthesis of research based on the implications for instruction of the science of learning summarized earlier (Deans for Impact 2015).

1. Develop a well sequenced curriculum with a clear progression which provides the necessary pre-requisites to master new ideas, and map new ideas onto ideas students already know. In the world course we mapped backward from competencies to knowledge, skills, and dispositions, and from those learning outcomes to smaller pedagogical units with partial learning outcomes that would gradually and over time build up the learning outcomes orienting the entire curriculum. We then integrated those smaller pedagogical units into sequences, which progressed with horizontal and vertical coherence—coherence within and between grades. Each unit was coded identifying the competencies it was intended to develop. Once we finished the design of the curriculum in this manner we "audited" the curriculum examining each of the 350 units for opportunities to develop each of the intended knowledge, skills, and dispositions, as presented in the framework, which guided the development of the curriculum. While we did not expect to include opportunities to develop each of the intended competencies in every unit, we did look for multiple, repeated, opportunities to foster such development across the years. This audit helped us identify gaps in the curriculum, where there were very limited opportunities to build a skill, as well as develop a structured sequence, where at any level in the progression we could ascertain that students had the opportunity to gain the pre-requisite knowledge. The sequence of the units progressed from what was known and immediate to the student toward more abstract ideas and concepts. For example, in the second grade, students began describing the games they played (immediate knowledge and interest), they then compared their interests within the classroom. Then they interviewed their parents about the games they played as children, and used these data to discuss changes over time in the games played by children, and variation across families and cultures. Then they engaged with peers in another country, using technology, comparing the games they all played. From this set of immediate observations and analyses, children then studied the similarities and differences in how various children experienced childhood across societies and generations.

   This approach to curriculum design builds on what is known about how students learn new ideas, by reference to ideas they know and presenting new information in a graduated way which allows them to transfer information from working memory to long term memory. The design of the curriculum challenged the conventional wisdom that cognitive development progresses through fixed sequences of stages, and instead was designed with appropriate instructional sequences designed to allow the mastery of new concepts.

2. Assume students can learn many different things, if well taught. Don't assume they are not "developmentally ready" to understand certain ideas. When we engage students with real world problems, some may assume that there is a developmental readiness for certain topics. When we were developing the World Course we debated with colleagues in a school who had first committed to teaching it issues such as whether second graders could learn about "poverty." Cognitive science establishes that development does not progress through a fixed stages sequence, and that good sequencing of design can support students as they learn about complex topics.
3. Develop units and lessons which make explicit why what students are learning is important, we adopted this approach in the development of the world course because it is known that this is one of the ways to facilitate recall of information.
4. Provide multiple opportunities for students to demonstrate their understanding and to receive feedback on their emerging understandings. When possible, provide extended opportunities for repeated practice over long periods. One of the established cognitive principles is that practice is essential to learning new content, and that practice extended over time and using multiple forms of practice is more effective to learning.

Design curriculum so it can help students solve problems by teaching different sets of facts at different ages in a logical progression. Create opportunities for students to demonstrate understanding that can provide students with feedback that is specific and clear, focused on the task, and explanatory. This is the role of formative assessment, described in the World Course as follows:

> From kindergarten, students not only learn but also are engaged in *demonstrating* their understanding of what they've learned throughout the year. We integrated formative and summative assessments into the course because we believe that global competency and twenty-first-century learning require authentic forms of assessment (Greenstein 2012). More than merely displaying knowledge, students are asked to engage in creating a product, whether that product is a puppet show (kindergarten), a book (first grade), a business plan (third grade), a game (fourth grade), or a social enterprise (eighth grade). Learning is constructed as *cumulative,* with knowledge building on prior experience and understanding. For example, in third grade, students learn to understand global interdependence through participating in creating a social-enterprise project in chocolate manufacturing. The learning objective is to build an entrepreneurial spirit in young children through an understanding of global food chains and the ethics of free trade and child labor using the case of chocolate. The primary geographic focus is on West Africa's chocolate-manufacturing countries. (Reimers et al. 2016, p. lxxiii)

5. Facilitate transfer of learning to new situations in or outside of classrooms by ensuring that students have the necessary background knowledge to understand the context of a problem and by presenting multiple examples which can help students understand the underlying structure of the problem they address.
6. Activate student motivation by fostering beliefs that ability can be improved through hard work, praising student effort and strategies and encouraging them to set learning goals (improvement rather than competence). Cultivate student intrinsic motivation by working around students' interests. Provide students

opportunities to monitor their own thinking and learning. Foster a sense of inclusion for students of all identities and abilities.

A curriculum can include structured opportunities for reflection in which students make visible how they think about their own learning. There are multiple ways in which a curriculum can foster a sense of inclusion, the most immediate, devising lessons in which students are invited to bring their experience, culture, and identities. In the World Course, for example, diversity is celebrated beginning in kindergarten. The overarching theme of kindergarten is "Our world is diverse and beautiful." Through activities in which students interview their parents—for example about the games parents played as children—or in which parents are invited to share their biographies and experiences in school, the curriculum conveys to all students that they "belong" in the school. Intentionally creating conditions that foster this sense of belonging is not only essential so all students can thrive, it can help all students develop the necessary skills to create those environments in the future.

Similarly valuable guidance to design curriculum and pedagogy can be drawn from scientific knowledge of how to support socio-emotional development. A US National Commission on social, emotional and academic development convened by the Aspen Institute, produced a series of recommendations based on the existing scientific evidence on socio-emotional development. The report recommends organizing instruction in ways which foster the integration between (1) skills and competencies, (2) attitudes, beliefs, and mindsets, and (3) character and values. Skills and competencies include: cognitive, social and interpersonal, and emotional. These develop and are used in interaction with attitudes, beliefs, and mindsets that children have about themselves, others, and their circumstances. They are also developed and used in interaction with character and values (Aspen Institute 2019, p. 15). This report underscores that developing these various competencies is essential not only because doing so is in service of academic learning, but because these outcomes (identity, motivation, character, and values) are important themselves. Drawing on evidence that social, emotional, and cognitive skills can be taught, the report recommends that they are taught explicitly (Ibid, p. 19). The kind of integration between cognitive, social, and emotional instruction which the report calls for will require significant redesign of teaching and learning. Beginning this process in the domain of global education is one way to carve space during the school day to more intentionally engage students in learning in ways that seek this interaction. As already mentioned, the units of the World Course were designed from the outset to address cognitive and socio-emotional skills. Similarly, the learning objectives guide aligned to the UN Sustainable Development Goals explicitly identifies cognitive, social and emotional objectives.

There are additional specialized bodies of research on cognitive and socio-emotional development which can support specific elements of a global education curriculum. For example, one of the important goals of global education is to help students develop the capacity for ethical reasoning. Lawrence Kohlberg, a pioneering figure in the study of moral development, expanding on the earlier work of Jean Piaget, established that moral development, which proceeds through a staged process, can be supported by providing students opportunities to discuss moral dilemmas. Kohlberg saw moral development as the result of social interaction and argued that as individuals faced cognitive conflicts at their current stage of moral development this would help them develop to a higher stage of morality (Kohlberg 1984). A global education curriculum can include many lessons which engage students in moral deliberation. In the World Course, for example, students learn about global interdependence in the third grade by studying the process of chocolate manufacturing in eight units: 1. Setting the Stage for the Life of a Chocolate; 2. The Life of a Chocolate and Its History; 3. Let's Make Our Own Chocolate; 4. Understanding the Culture of My Market; 5. Marketing My Chocolate in School; 6. Child Labor; 7. Taking My Chocolate to the Market; and 8. Beyond Chocolate. These units engage them in multiple opportunities for moral deliberation, for example when discussing child labor and fair trade.

One of the purposes of a global education curriculum is to help students value differences across multiple lines of identity, such as race, ethnicity, culture, religion, and nationality and to communicate across those lines of difference. There is a robust body of knowledge from socio-psychological research which can inform sensible design of curriculum and activities aligned with those goals. Research on intergroups relations falls into three approaches. First, social identity theory posits that people sort themselves into "we" and "they" categories, and that this process can engender bias as people extend preferences to their in-groups. Competition for scarce resources and perceived threats turns in-group favoritism to harming competing groups. Second, social categorization is when the use of social categories activates stereotypes and prejudice leading to discrimination. Finally, social dominance theory is where the hierarchical arrangement of racial categories is maintained through various institutions (Richeson and Sommers 2016, pp. 445–447).

An implication of this socio-psychological research showing that it is the use of social categories that leads to discrimination is that curriculum can help students problematize categories, for example challenging notions of a "single story" which reduce members of "out-groups" to a singular identity, and developing a curiosity about all groups that can help understand the multidimensional nature of identity and find common humanity across identity groups. The popular TED talk by writer Chimamanda Ngozi "The danger of the single story" is an example of a resource that can help students reflect upon and begin a conversation about how to think in more nuanced ways about those whom they perceive to be different and about identity (Adichie 2009). Similarly, curriculum can help students reflect on the way in which multiple dimensions define identity and understand the concept of intersectionality (Gold and Grant 1977). Finally, curriculum can help students identify and question racial hierarchies and the mechanisms through which they are perpetuated. For instance, the World Course fifth grade curriculum focuses on social change to advance the rights of individuals, examining the American, French and Haitian revolutions, the abolition of Apartheid in South Africa, as well as the global movement for Universal Human Rights. The seventh-grade curriculum examines the civil rights movement in the United States, the women's movement and the environmental movement.

Research also shows that there are positive benefits from intergroup relations in terms of reducing prejudice and discrimination (Brown and Hewstone 2005; Pettigrew and Tropp 2006). The seminal work of psychologist Allport (1954) on intergroup contact identified optimal conditions for such interactions as characterized by equal status, cooperation, and common goals and support from authorities, but subsequent research documents benefit even in the absence of those optimal conditions (Hewstone et al. 2014).

There are many ways in which curriculum can promote these types of exchanges. The first is structuring diverse schools and classrooms, where students experience diversity as a matter of daily life. It is also possible to expose students to diversity in the content of the curriculum, for example, in the selection of readings available in language and literature classes, including readings from diverse authors, as well as readings that explicitly examine the different experiences and perspectives of different groups. Courses in social studies can also directly engage students in the study of inter-race or intergroup relations, and can help increase their literacy in various cultures. For example, students could study various religious traditions, essential knowledge in a world in which many people make sense of the world through a religious lens. Results from the Pew Research organization show that there is significant religious ignorance among Americans, even though most Americans say that religion is very important in their lives. On average, adults can answer about half of the questions in a survey designed to assess basic knowledge of various religious traditions. While most Americans have familiarity with the basics of Christianity, and know some facts about Islam, very few are knowledgeable about Judaism, Hinduism, or Buddhism. Those who know people of other faiths have greater knowledge, and those who are more knowledgeable have more favorable views of other religious groups (Alper 2019).

Curriculum can also organize activities that extend the interactions of students with peers from different countries and cultures, such as through the use of technology and through student travel and exchanges.

As curriculum provides students opportunities to directly study the topic of race, the diverse experiences of different racial groups over time in different societies, and inter-race relations, it is helpful that such study is informed by current sociopsychological research which underscores race primarily as a product of dynamic social construction, and not a predetermined biological fact (Richeson and Sommers 2016, p. 441). Perceived status, health and psychosocial factors such as prejudice, group identification, stereotypes, political ideology, and beliefs about race shape the racial category to which individuals are assigned (Ibid, p. 443).

Another area where the science of learning can support global education concerns research on how adults learn, as it can help design opportunities for teachers, school leaders, and other administrators to develop the necessary skills to advance global education. In studying how adults learn Robert Kegan and Lisa Lahey have discovered that pre-existing habits and mindsets often prevent acting on new knowledge. They have found that if adults can be made aware of how those pre-existing beliefs and assumptions are getting in the way they can more readily change and accept change in their organizations (Kegan and Lahey 2009).

Any effort to introduce global education in an existing school will have to meet adults where they are. Teachers and leaders are not blank slates, they come with their pre-existing beliefs and commitments, some of which may not immediately embrace global education. A study of social studies teachers in Indiana emphasizes the need for teacher knowledge and the challenges of accommodating global education to their curriculum (Rapoport 2010). These teachers reported never using the term "global citizenship." A study of teachers in England found that even among those who thought global education was important, very few had confidence in their ability to teach it (Davies et al. in Yamashita 2006). A comparative study of the practice of global education in four countries found that teachers needed significantly more time to agree upon and develop strategies for global education (Osler and Vincent 2002). A study of the implementation of global education in various Canadian provinces found that administrators' beliefs clashed with the inclusion of global education in the primary school curriculum, resulting in a lack of support to schools to build curriculum and professional capacity:

> Despite increasingly strong inclusion of global education in the formal curricula, most officials we interviewed in education ministries and school boards across Canada viewed global education activities as an optional rather than a mandatory activity. Indeed, a significant number of the educational administrators in our sample expressed skepticism about the appropriateness of introducing global education themes at the elementary school level. (Mundy and Manion 2008, p. 956)

Too often, competing or unclear definitions of what global competency is or how to achieve it are the reason for lack of pedagogical action. Because much of the debate about global education remains academic and abstract, a conversation for the initiated and disconnected from practice, it fails to include the uninitiated or to engage the novice productively. A productive way to engage teachers in these conversations is in the context of a practice of global education, using the practice as an opportunity to test emerging understandings, for instance of alternative views of global education, and to refine them as they engage in a practice of teaching a global curriculum. In my work with teachers and leaders, I have found it productive to engage them as teams in a thirteen-step school-wide process to develop and implement a global education program. The process begins with a discussion of what a high school graduate should know, care about and be able to do to achieve an ambitious goal such as the elimination of poverty. From that discussion, teams move to a more specific conversation about the kinds of pedagogical sequences that can help students develop those competencies. Such processes for collaborative work in schools provide a context in which some of the barriers created by conceptual disagreements may surface and be addressed, providing opportunities for clarification, learning, and negotiation (Reimers et al. 2018, 2019).

Some years ago, as I was working with the entire staff of an independent school in a workshop following this process, the chair of the science department came to see me after the workshop had concluded to thank me. He had been resisting the school leader's efforts to develop a school-wide program of global education and explained that the workshop, and in particular collaborating with his colleagues in designing lesson plans, had helped him understand for the first time that global education was not an alternative to the traditional subjects, but that it was a way to integrate the existing traditional subjects and to help students work on real world problems. "Now that I see that there is plenty of room for science education in this program, I am more ready to embrace it." He said, In my practice, I have found that competing definitions of what global education is and entails are common barriers for a coherent schoolwide program of global education when the discussion is too abstract and unrelated to actual instructional practice.

Because teachers are not blank slates when they engage with global education, pre-existing views may be more or less supportive to global education. A survey of teachers in a network of high schools working to advance global citizenship in Denmark identified differences in the extent to which teachers in different subjects believed they understood the concept of global citizenship. Science and math teachers were, on average, less confident than teachers in language arts or in social studies. Science teachers were also found to be less interested in global education, 30% of them did not see the relevance of global education for their subjects, compared to 8% among social science teachers and 11% of the language arts teachers. These quotes from teachers interviewed in that study are illustrative of those pre-existing mindsets:

> I think it takes a little developing for some, typically it is said that the science subjects have a harder time figuring out where the global dimension fits in. But I think, especially in cooperation with others, it is possible. (Nilsson 2015, p. 25)
>
> I think maybe, without pointing fingers at anyone, that for example a Math teacher here at the school, or a physics teacher my age would say 'what kind of nonsense is this, they need to learn some formulas and quadratic equations'. (Nilsson 2015, p. 34)

The mindset that global education "belongs" in social studies is pervasive and can hamper efforts for interdisciplinary collaboration. A study of the implementation of global education in seven provinces in Canada found a similar concentration of global education in social studies. The notion of infusing global education across the curriculum was not reflected in the standards (Mundy and Manion 2008, p. 953).

References

Adichie, C. N. (2009). *The danger of a single story*. Ted Global. https://www.ted.com/talks/chimamanda_adichie_the_danger_of_a_single_story?language=en.

Allport, G. W. (1954). *The nature of prejudice*. Addison-Wesley.

Alper, B. (2019). *6 facts about what Americans know about religion*. Pew Research Center. https://www.pewresearch.org/fact-tank/2019/07/23/6-facts-about-what-americans-know-about-religion/.

Aspen Institute. (2019). National Commission on Social, Emotional and Academic Development. *From a nation at risk to a nation at Hope*. https://www.aspeninstitute.org/programs/national-commission-on-social-emotional-and-academic-development/

Brown, R., & Hewstone, M. (2005). An integrative theory of intergroup contact. In M. P. Zanna (Ed.), *Advances in experimental social psychology* (pp 255–343). San Diego, CA: Academic. https://www.businessinsider.com/bill-gates-foundation-helps-invent-tiger-toilets-powered-by-worms-2019-1.

Deans for Impact. (2015). *The science of learning*. Austin, TX: Deans for Impact.

Gold, M. J., & Grant, C. A. (1977). In praise of diversity: A resource book for multicultural education. Publications Archives, 1963-2000. 66. https://digitalcommons.unomaha.edu/cparpubarchives/66.

Hewstone, M., Lolliot, S., Swart, H., Myers, E., Voci, A., et al. (2014). Intergroup contact and intergroup conflict. *Journal of Peace Pschology., 20,* 39–53.

Kegan, R., & Lahey, L. (2009). *Immunity to change: How to overcome it and unlock the potential in yourself and your organization (Leadership for the Common Good)*. Cambridge, MA: Harvard Business Press.

Kohlberg, L. (1984). *The psychology of moral development: The nature and validity of moral stages* (Essays on Moral Development, Volume 2). Harper & Row.

Mundy, K., & Manion, C. (2008). Global education in Canadian elementary schools: An exploratory study. *Canadian Journal of Education, 31*(4), 941–974.

Nilsson, I. (2015). *Understanding global education–a case study of the global high schools Nework in Denmark*. Lund University. Department of Sociology. Undergraduate thesis. http://lup.lub.lu.se/luur/download?func=downloadFile&recordOId=5469540&fileOId=5469541.

Osler, A., & Vincent, K. (2002). *Citizenship and the challenge of global education*. Staffordshire, England: Trentham Books.

Pellegrino, J. W., & Hilton, M. L. (Eds.). (2012). *Education for life and work: Developing transferable knowledge and skills in the 21st century*. Washington, DC: The National Academies Press.

Pettigrew, T. F., & Tropp, L. R. (2006). A meta-analytic test of intergroup contact theory. *Journal of Personality and Social Psychology, 90,* 751–783.

Rapoport, A. (2010). We cannot teach what we don't know: Indiana teachers talk about global citizenship education. *Education, Citizenship and Social Justice, 5*(3), 179–190.

Reimers, F., Chopra, V., Chung, C., Higdon, J., & O'Donnell, E. B. (2016). *Empowering global citizens*. Charleston, SC: CreateSpace.

Reimers, F., Adams, R., & Shannon, K. (2018). *Twelve lessons to open classrooms and minds to the world*. Washington, DC: The NEA Foundation.

Reimers, F., Adams, R., & Berka, M. (2019). *Creative lessons to open classrooms and minds to the world*. Washington, DC: The NEA Foundation.

Richeson, J., & Sommers, S. (2016). Toward a social psychology of race and race relations for the twenty-first century. *Annual Review of Psychology, 67,* 439–463.

Yamashita, H. (2006). Global citizenship education and war. The needs of teachers and learners. *Educational Review, 58*(1), 27–39.

Open Access This chapter is licensed under the terms of the Creative Commons Attribution 4.0 International License (http://creativecommons.org/licenses/by/4.0/), which permits use, sharing, adaptation, distribution and reproduction in any medium or format, as long as you give appropriate credit to the original author(s) and the source, provide a link to the Creative Commons license and indicate if changes were made.

The images or other third party material in this chapter are included in the chapter's Creative Commons license, unless indicated otherwise in a credit line to the material. If material is not included in the chapter's Creative Commons license and your intended use is not permitted by statutory regulation or exceeds the permitted use, you will need to obtain permission directly from the copyright holder.

Chapter 5
A Professional Perspective and Global Education

As described earlier, a professional perspective recognizes the importance of using expert knowledge to guide educational practice. There are two implications of this perspective for the development of a program of global education, the first is the need to provide teachers access to extant expert knowledge, helping them develop as professionals, for example engaging teachers in the study of the various intellectual traditions that undergird global education, or increasing their knowledge of climate change, and examining the implications of this knowledge for practice. The second implication is that teachers themselves should contribute to develop expert knowledge in global education, something they could do as they engage in the practice of global education.

Curriculum is not self-executing. A quality program of global education will require teachers with the expertise to teach that curriculum. A recent survey of a nationally representative sample of science teachers in the United States conducted by the National Center for Science Education revealed that whereas three-quarters of the teachers address climate change in their classes, only half of them to do in ways that are aligned with the current scientific consensus. When asked to rate their own content knowledge with respect to climate change, ecology, modern genetics, weather forecasting, and health and nutrition, 17% of the teachers report that they know less about this topic that most other high school teachers, and 31% report the same for weather forecasting models. Only 28% of the teachers report that their knowledge of climate change is very good or exceptional, compared to 45% who report this level of knowledge for ecology or 44% for genetics or 48% for health and nutrition (Plutzer et al. 2016, p. 19). When asked to select a series of possible topics to be covered to teach a unit on greenhouse gases and recent global warming, a topic which most teachers reported they taught and one on which the basic science on how these gases trap heat is a century old and noncontroversial, only some of the teachers selected as high priority topics which are essential to understand greenhouse gases: 74% for carbon dioxide trapping, 59% use of coal and oil by utility companies, 56% emissions from industry, 55% destruction of forests; in contrast, a number of teachers selected as high priority topics which are not relevant to understanding greenhouse gases: 42% depletion of ozone in the upper atmosphere, 24% incoming

© The Author(s) 2020
F. M. Reimers, *Educating Students to Improve the World*,
SpringerBriefs in Education, https://doi.org/10.1007/978-981-15-3887-2_5

shortwave and outgoing longwave energy, 23% use of chemicals as pesticides, 21% people heating and cooking in their homes, 14% use of aerosol spray cans, and 4% launching rockets into space (Ibid, p. 21). The same survey reveals that many teachers are unaware of the scientific consensus attributing global warming to human activities, only 39% correctly identify that over 80% of climate scientists think that global warming is caused mostly by human activities, and only 21% of the teachers admit that they don't know the answer, the remaining 40% provide an incorrect answer (Ibid, p. 22). Teachers report that they have received very limited training on climate change, only 43% had any formal instruction on the subject at the college level, and only 10% completed a course on the subject (Ibid, p. 23). Among those without education on climate change during initial preparation, only 18% received any professional development on the subject. Teachers recognize this topic as a high need for preparation, and 67% report that they would be interested in professional development opportunities on the subject (Ibid, p. 24).

5.1 Helping Teachers Gain Knowledge and Skills in Global Education

Studies on deeper learning and twenty-first-century skills emphasize the importance of building teacher capacity to translate twenty-first-century curriculum into effective instruction as a significant challenge as well as a priority. The National Research Council Report calls for significant changes in teacher preparation:

> Current systems of teacher preparation and professional development will require major changes if they are to support teaching that encourages deeper learning and the development of transferable competencies. Changes will need to be made not only in conceptions of what constitutes effective professional practice but also in the purposes, structure, and organization of preservice and professional learning opportunities. (Pellegrino and Hilton 2012, p. 186)

Similarly, the US National Commission on social, emotional and academic development underscores the urgency of the professional development challenge, calling for the redesign of educator preparation programs, collaborative decision-making in schools and districts; the prioritization of social, emotional, and cognitive skills and competencies in recruitment, hiring, orientation, and professional learning; incentivizing innovation in teacher preparation programs; redesigning licensure and accreditation; ensuring that induction programs for new teachers support these domains; and restructured adult workforce systems (Aspen Institute 2019, pp. 50–53).

Teachers need to not only develop knowledge and skills in global education, but also develop shared understandings with colleagues within their schools to be able to collaborate in the design and implementation of a coherent and rigorous curriculum which extends across grades and subjects beyond a few lessons on global topics here and there. A study of teachers in a network of schools in Denmark which were committed to advancing global education found important variability in understandings of what global education was and in how it related to various subjects across teachers in these schools (Nilsson 2015). These various conceptualizations include education that is global, including understanding interconnectedness and interdependency, the process of globalization, and themes like climate change and migration. The second conceptualization of global education encompassed understanding and respecting other cultures and people and gaining competencies to live in a global world. Finally, a third conceptualization described global education as teacher and school work, emphasizing the need for a coordinated approach and sharing resources at the school, as well as the different challenges of integrating global education in various subjects (Nilsson 2015, p. 31).

In a study of curriculum reforms in Chile, China, India, Mexico, Singapore, and the United States, we found that as more ambitious goals were embraced by states and countries, the topic of teacher education and professional development received greater priority (Reimers and Chung 2016). A comparative study of programs of teacher professional development that focused on supporting teachers in developing the capacities to educate the whole child in Chile, China, Colombia, India, Mexico, Singapore, and the United States, identified that they shared the following characteristics:

1. These professional development programs reflect a conception of adult learning that sees it as socially situated and responding to the current needs of teachers for learning.
2. This form of professional development involves sustained and extensive opportunities for teachers to build capacities, often extending an entire school year, or spanning across multiple school years, that contrasts with the more prevalent opportunities of short courses out of the school.
3. The modalities of professional development examined in this book are varied. They include independent study of new material, discussion with peers and others, individual or group coaching, demonstrations of new practices, independent research projects, and opportunities for reflection.
4. The curriculum of the programs examined covers a blend of capacities, from a broad focus on helping students develop capacities to a highly granular identification of particular pedagogies and instructional practices that can help students gain those skills.
5. The curriculum of these various programs reflects a view of learning which includes cognitive skills, in interaction with dispositions and socio-emotional skills.
6. Professional development includes exposure to visible routines, protocols and instructional practices, where teachers see in practice new forms of instruction or assessment.
7. These programs rely on a mix of opportunities for learning situated in the context of the schools where teachers work.

8. To support the intensive and sustained activities of professional development that these various programs advance, the organizations in charge build a range of partnerships with institutions outside of schools that contribute various types of resources.
9. These programs see teacher practice as situated in specific organizations and social contexts, and in general adopt a whole-school approach, rather than helping individual teachers increase their capacity.
10. The question of measurement. These programs all develop capacities among teachers to advance pedagogies with the goal of developing competencies that are not formally assessed in the school or school system. In this sense, the programs challenge the notion that "What gets measured gets done," and suggest that teachers can make decisions about what and how to teach that can transcend the formal accountability structures in the school.
11. The organizations that support these various programs all model a learning orientation. They approach schools with an inquiry mindset, engage in dialogue with school staff about their learning goals, use various forms of feedback to assess whether their work is achieving the intended results, and implement measures to course correct and generate continuous improvement in their work (Reimers 2018).

These features of high-quality professional development programs can be replicated in programs to increase the level of expertise of teachers for global education. Some of these principles were reflected in a book I wrote, with my graduate students, to help disseminate the approach to global education curriculum we had followed in developing the World Course. When the book *Empowering Global Citizens* was published in 2016 I began to receive feedback that underscored the need to support the development of teacher capacities to design and teach this kind of curriculum, aligned with an ambitious framework of competencies, in turn, aligned to the UN Sustainable Development Goals.

To address this need I developed, in collaboration with 36 of my graduate students, a resource book which included a protocol to establish a school-wide process of global education, that explained how to develop curriculum aligned with the UN Sustainable Development Goals, and that illustrated with a small number of lessons what this curriculum could look like in practice (Reimers et al. 2017). The proposed thirteen-step process recognized the importance of creating a process specific to the school which would help teams of teachers collaborate in developing a shared vision for global education, develop a curriculum prototype, and learn from experience. The protocol also suggested that schools sought to join networks with other schools following a similar process, as a way to accelerate the learning opportunities resulting from their shared experience in attempting similar goals. The steps proposed in this process were:

1. Establish a leadership team. This team will form the guiding coalition that will design and manage the implementation of the whole-school global citizenship education strategy.

5.1 Helping Teachers Gain Knowledge and Skills in Global Education

2. Develop a long-term vision. What are the long-term outcomes for students, for the school and for the communities that these graduates will influence that inspire this effort?
3. Develop a framework of knowledge, skills, and dispositions for graduates of the school that is aligned with the long-term vision.
4. Audit existing curriculum in the school in light of the proposed long-term vision and global competencies framework.
5. Design a prototype to better align the existing curriculum to the global competencies framework in step 3 (the sixty lessons presented in this book can serve as an initial prototype, or as a sacrificial proposal that leads to the prototype a particular school adopts).
6. Communicate vision, framework and prototype to the extended community in the school, seek feedback, and iterate.
7. Decide on a revised prototype to be implemented and develop an implementation plan to execute the global education prototype.
8. Identify resources necessary and available to implement the global education prototype.
9. Develop a framework to monitor implementation of the prototype and obtain formative feedback.
10. Develop a communication strategy to build and maintain support from key stakeholders.
11. Develop a professional development strategy.
12. Execute the prototype with oversight and support of the leadership team.
13. Evaluate the execution of the prototype, adjust as necessary, and go back to step 4.

This process sees the task of creating a global education curriculum as an opportunity for professional development, based in the school, and the collaboration among teachers in developing, teaching and evaluating this curriculum as a means to build their own expertise in doing so, as a result of experimentation. In effect, the process is designed to build the capacities of teachers to advance global education as they embark on designing and implementing a school-wide program of global education. The approach is built on the premise that all learning requires an opportunity to practice, and that it is the reflection on that practice that helps develop new knowledge and skills. Essentially, teaching any curriculum is based on two hypotheses: If we teach A students will learn B, and if students learn B outcomes C, D, and E will be achieved for them and for their communities. Most teachers do not formally test their hypotheses, much less do so publicly. The process I devised is one that allows teachers to work within a transparent framework that helps them make the hypotheses they are testing visible and to learn from that process. As teachers do this work in collaboration with their colleagues in a school-wide process, this helps build shared knowledge about what works well, in other words, it builds shared professional expertise.

As schools join others in improvement networks, these networks of schools become a means to augment the collective capacity of the participating schools and also their access to expertise resident in the network. This, in turn, augments the capacity to test the hypotheses underlying any curriculum. This is what Tony Bryk and his colleagues have called "improvement networks," adapting to the field of education well-established principles of the field of improvement science (Bryk et al. 2015).

I have found that engaging teachers in collaborative work discussing the relationship between curriculum, pedagogy and big global challenges such as how to build a world that is inclusive and sustainable resonates with deep values for many teachers. Many teachers joined the profession in order to make a contribution to society and have a lasting impact on their students' development. This is shown by Table 5.1 which presents data from an OECD survey administered to teachers which asked what were the reasons teachers joined the profession. Most teachers across the world reply that their motives included influencing the development of children, benefit the disadvantaged and contributing to society. Engaging teachers in the design of curriculum to "improve the world" taps into this powerful intrinsic motivation of many teachers.

5.2 Engaging Teachers as Creators of Expert Knowledge in Global Education

The process described above, of school-based innovation with the support of a school network, is one that simultaneously recognizes teachers as experts of the process of curricular innovation, while engaging them in a learning community that further develops that expertise and enables them to create knowledge based on practice.

In *The Reflective Practitioner*, a classic book on professional practice and education, Donald Schon argues that the ability to reflect on the knowledge which guides practice is essential to the improvement of professional practice (Schon 1983). A reflective practitioner "turns thought back on action and on the knowing which is implicit in action." While trying to make sense of an action, a reflective practitioner "reflects on the understandings which have been explicit in his action, understandings which he surfaces, criticizes, restructures, and embodies in further action" (Schon 1983). Practitioners often guide their practice with problem-solving knowledge that goes beyond the mechanic application of principles or conclusions drawn from basic science. Schon also argues that the failure to comprehend this all too often leads institutions involved in professional education to base the curriculum on a paradigm which assumes that professional practice is simply the application of the general principles drawn from basic research in the field to problems of practice. I share Schon's view that such a paradigm is limited and insufficient to fully support effective professional practice, particularly when professionals encounter "messy problems."

This epistemological stance recognizes that when practitioners solve problems they learn from the consequences of their actions, and the knowledge they gain makes them better at solving problems in the future, hence better professionals.

Table 5.1 Motivation to join the profession, by teachers' teaching experience. *Results based on responses of lower secondary teachers*

	Teaching allowed me to influence the development of children and young people		Teaching allowed me to benefit the socially disadvantaged		Teaching allowed me to provide a contribution to society	
	Total		Total		Total	
	%	S.E.	%	S.E.	%	S.E.
Alberta (Canada)	98.8	(0.4)	77.8	(2.2)	94.7	(1.1)
Australia	96.0	(0.4)	79.8	(0.7)	92.6	(0.5)
Austria	95.6	(0.3)	75.3	(0.7)	87.1	(0.6)
Belgium	95.5	(0.3)	70.3	(0.8)	86.3	(0.6)
– *Flemish Comm. (Belgium)*	96.7	(0.3)	77.0	(1.0)	91.9	(0.5)
Brazil	95.4	(0.5)	93.7	(0.6)	97.2	(0.3)
Bulgaria	94.5	(0.6)	64.5	(1.0)	92.3	(0.6)
CABA (Argentina)	86.2	(1.0)	74.6	(1.1)	91.5	(0.8)
Chile	96.7	(0.4)	94.4	(0.7)	97.8	(0.4)
Colombia	98.2	(0.4)	95.8	(0.7)	98.8	(0.3)
Croatia	95.3	(0.4)	79.6	(0.7)	91.3	(0.5)
Cyprus	94.7	(0.6)	86.4	(1.1)	94.6	(0.7)
Czech Republic	92.6	(0.5)	67.9	(0.9)	89.0	(0.6)
Denmark	94.2	(0.6)	64.1	(1.2)	75.7	(1.1)
England (UK)	97.2	(0.4)	81.4	(1.2)	92.5	(0.6)
Estonia	87.5	(0.8)	62.3	(1.2)	81.8	(0.8)
Finland	82.7	(0.8)	59.5	(1.0)	65.6	(0.9)
France	92.1	(0.5)	70.3	(0.9)	83.1	(0.7)
Georgia	97.0	(0.4)	85.4	(1.0)	96.4	(0.4)
Hungary	92.7	(0.5)	69.2	(1.3)	84.4	(0.9)
Iceland	78.7	(1.2)	57.4	(1.4)	80.2	(1.2)
Israel	96.7	(0.4)	91.0	(0.8)	96.0	(0.4)
Italy	78.5	(0.7)	85.8	(0.6)	93.8	(0.4)
Japan	89.0	(0.6)	66.3	(0.9)	81.6	(0.7)
Kazakhstan	93.9	(0.4)	78.0	(0.7)	92.5	(0.5)
Korea	88.4	(0.6)	72.7	(0.8)	79.7	(0.9)
Latvia	93.2	(0.6)	80.0	(1.0)	92.6	(0.5)
Lithuania	91.4	(0.4)	71.5	(0.9)	85.5	(0.6)
Malta	96.3	(0.5)	84.2	(0.9)	92.8	(0.8)
Mexico	98.8	(0.2)	93.9	(0.5)	98.2	(0.3)

(continued)

Table 5.1 (continued)

	Teaching allowed me to influence the development of children and young people		Teaching allowed me to benefit the socially disadvantaged		Teaching allowed me to provide a contribution to society	
	Total		Total		Total	
	%	S.E.	%	S.E.	%	S.E.
Netherlands	86.1	(1.4)	41.6	(2.3)	80.1	(1.5)
New Zealand	95.8	(0.5)	80.4	(1.2)	92.5	(0.6)
Norway	88.9	(0.5)	61.2	(1.0)	79.1	(0.7)
Portugal	94.0	(0.4)	90.2	(0.4)	93.2	(0.4)
Romania	98.1	(0.2)	89.0	(0.7)	96.0	(0.4)
Russia	88.1	(0.7)	80.7	(0.9)	90.9	(0.7)
Saudi Arabia	94.0	(0.6)	90.6	(0.7)	92.9	(0.6)
Shanghai (China)	93.3	(0.4)	80.7	(0.8)	92.8	(0.5)
Singapore	97.8	(0.3)	88.4	(0.7)	95.4	(0.4)
Slovak Republic	93.2	(0.5)	61.6	(1.0)	92.3	(0.5)
Slovenia	88.8	(0.8)	60.5	(1.4)	86.8	(0.8)
South Africa	98.1	(0.4)	88.6	(1.1)	97.1	(0.5)
Spain	88.6	(0.6)	79.4	(0.7)	90.5	(0.5)
Sweden	93.5	(0.6)	77.7	(0.9)	86.8	(0.7)
Chinese Taipei	94.0	(0.4)	87.9	(0.6)	94.2	(0.4)
Turkey	97.8	(0.3)	91.1	(0.4)	98.3	(0.2)
United Arab Emirates	97.5	(0.2)	90.5	(0.4)	97.2	(0.2)
United States	98.7	(0.3)	83.8	(1.0)	96.5	(0.6)
Vietnam	98.8	(0.2)	95.2	(0.5)	98.7	(0.2)
OECD average-31	92.3	(0.1)	74.7	(0.2)	88.2	(0.1)
EU total-23	90.7	(0.2)	75.5	(0.3)	88.7	(0.2)
TALIS average-48	93.2	(0.1)	78.2	(0.1)	90.4	(0.1)

Source OECD (2019, Table I.4.1)

Solving problems, especially complex, messy, adaptive, or divergent problems, thus requires much more than mechanically applying lessons drawn from research to new situations, but involves forms of creation, design of solutions, and experimentation. While good professionals learn from these private experiments that constitute their practice, this knowledge is often accessible only to the practitioner, because it is not processed in a way that allows others to learn from it. This is called "tacit" knowledge.

Constructing opportunities to learn from such knowledge as in the thirteen-step process outlined earlier, transforms tacit knowledge into public knowledge and is critical to the development of global education as a professional practice.

Some of the most fundamental critiques to university-based professional education concern whether the curriculum provides sufficient access to knowledge essential for effective practice, and whether such university-based professional education remains too theoretical and disconnected from the fields of practice for which it is preparing individuals. These critiques resonate with the dissociation I described at the outset of this book between the scholarly literature on global education and the practice-based literature.

Donald Schon in *The Reflective Practitioner* argues that the classical model that assumes that practice is the mere application of foundational principles in applied contexts is responsible for this disconnect. It is not uncommon to hear voices from various fields of practice state that the deficiencies of professional preparation require that novices are taught what they need to know in the first years of professional practice. This challenge is compounded as technological change has increased the demands for professional practice in most fields, making clear that initial professional preparation is but one step in a long trajectory of development, that should extend throughout the careers of most professionals. Life-long professional preparation is recognized as essential to support people in their careers, especially as they take on new assignments for which their previous preparation and experience does not sufficiently prepare them.

Using the book "Empowering Students to Improve the World in Sixty Lessons" as a starting point, I have worked with networks of teachers in developing global education curriculum, such as the Rete Dialogue, a network of teachers in Italy committed to democratic education, in translating and adapting this book to the Italian context. Over a year, this network of teachers translated the original book, taught these lessons, and then modified them, as part of a learning community in which they collaborated in this process across various regions in the country. The result of this process was a revised curriculum, reflecting the learning these teachers had drawn from their practice in experimenting with the original lessons (Reimers et al. 2018a).

Similarly, working with a group of fifty teacher leaders supported by the National Education Association Foundation in the United States, we developed a curriculum, inspired by "Empowering Students to Improve the World in Sixty Lessons" in which teams of teachers from all US states collaboratively designed grade-specific lessons aligned with the UN Sustainable Development Goals, taught them in their respective schools, and then improved based on their various experiences teaching them. This year-long collaborative project, relying on the use of communication technology, led to two publications developed with two different groups of teachers which they then used to further advance global education in their schools (Reimers et al. 2018b, 2019).

While this approach to professional development based on peer learning and networking is capacious and valued by teachers, it is relatively rare—only 44% of the teachers reported participating in it in the OECD study of teachers. This is low in comparison to 70% of teachers who report participating in traditional forms of professional development, such as courses or seminars (OECD 2019, p. 152).

Similar research-practice collaborative networks have been recommended to integrate cognitive and socio-emotional learning:

> Create research-practice partnerships to provide useful, actionable information for the field. Develop meaningful research-practice partnerships that engage researchers, school and program leaders, teachers and staff, policymakers and families and youth themselves in collaborative inquiry and learning. These multi-disciplinary teams should include people at various levels of the system and with diverse perspectives; focus on critical and immediate problems of practice that are important locally and have larger implications for the field; and use iterative inquiry cycles and collaborative data analysis to learn together and test out proposed changes. These findings from this research should be intentionally crafted to be relevant and accessible to educators and policymakers, such as through field-facing summaries and video. (Aspen Institute 2019, p. 63)

References

Aspen Institute. (2019). *From a nation at risk to a nation at hope.* National Commission on Social, Emotional and Academic Development. Retrieved form https://www.aspeninstitute.org/programs/national-commission-on-social-emotional-and-academic-development/.

Bryk, A., Gomez, L., Grunow, A., LeMahieu P. (2015). *Learning to Improve. How America's Schools Can Get Better at Getting Better.* Cambridge, MA: Harvard Education Press.

Nilsson, I. (2015). *Understanding global education—A case study of the global high schools network in Denmark.* Undergraduate thesis, Lund University, Department of Sociology. Retrieved form http://lup.lub.lu.se/luur/download?func=downloadFile&recordOId=5469540&fileOId=5469541.

OECD. (2019). *TALIS 2018 results. Volume I. Teachers and school leaders as lifelong learners.* Retrieved December 3, 2019, form http://www.oecd.org/education/talis/.

Pellegrino, J. W., & Hilton, M. L. (Eds.). (2012). *Education for life and work: Developing transferable knowledge and skills in the 21st century.* Washington, DC: The National Academies Press.

Plutzer, E., Lee Hannah, A., Rosenau, J., McCaffrey, M. S., Berbeco, M., & Reid, A. H. (2016). *Mixed messages: How climate is taught in America's schools.* Oakland, CA: National Center for Science Education. Retrieved form http://ncse.com/files/MixedMessages.pdf.

Reimers, F. (2018). A study in how teachers learn to educate whole students and how schools build the capacity to support them. In F. Reimers, & K. Chung (Eds.), *Preparing teachers to educate whole students: An international comparative study* (pp. 1–32). Cambridge, MA: Harvard Education Publishing.

Reimers, F., & Chung, C. (Eds.). (2016). *Teaching and learning for the twenty first century.* Cambridge: Harvard Education Press.

Reimers, F., et al. (2017). *Empowering students to improve the world in sixty lessons.* Charleston, SC: CreateSpace.

Reimers, F., Barzano, G., Fisichella, L., & Lissoni, M. (2018a). *Cittadinanza globale e sviluppo sostenibile.* Milan, Italy: Pearson.

Reimers, F., Adams, R., & Shannon, K. (2018b). *Twelve lessons to open classrooms and minds to the world.* Washington, DC: The NEA Foundation.

Reimers, F., Adams, R., & Berka, M. (2019). *Creative lessons to open classrooms and minds to the world.* Washington, DC: The NEA Foundation.

Schon, D. (1983). *The reflective practitioner: How professionals think in action.* New York: Basic Books.

Open Access This chapter is licensed under the terms of the Creative Commons Attribution 4.0 International License (http://creativecommons.org/licenses/by/4.0/), which permits use, sharing, adaptation, distribution and reproduction in any medium or format, as long as you give appropriate credit to the original author(s) and the source, provide a link to the Creative Commons license and indicate if changes were made.

The images or other third party material in this chapter are included in the chapter's Creative Commons license, unless indicated otherwise in a credit line to the material. If material is not included in the chapter's Creative Commons license and your intended use is not permitted by statutory regulation or exceeds the permitted use, you will need to obtain permission directly from the copyright holder.

Chapter 6
An Institutional Perspective and Global Education

Adopting an institutional perspective to advance a program of global education leads to identifying the norms, structures, organization, and elements of the system which can support global education. Those elements include standards and curriculum, instructional resources, assessments, staff and development, school organization, governance, and funding. Key in this perspective is seeking alignment and coherence between these various elements of the system.

> Realizing the vision of deeper, transferable knowledge for all students will require complementary changes across the many elements that make up the public education system. These elements include curriculum, instruction, assessment, and teacher preparation and professional development. (Pellegrino and Hilton 2012, 186)

A study of the implementation of global education in elementary schools in five provinces in Canada illustrates what happens when these elements are not well aligned. The authors found variation across provinces in the explicit focus on global education in the standards and that, even when the standards included global education as a curricular goal, there was very limited support offered by provincial ministries and education departments, so schools were left to their own devices to design curriculum. Provincial administrators largely saw global education as a non-essential, particularly at the elementary school level. Schools established partnerships with NGOs to receive support in global education, but the quality varied across schools, with many limited to one-off activities which engaged students in fundraising efforts. The result was great variation across schools and teachers in how global education was understood, and large gaps between the standards and the activities which took place in schools. Most of the standards emphasized knowledge of facts, rather than actionable aspects of global challenges (Mundy and Manion 2008).

UNESCO's survey to governments to assess the extent of adoption of the recommendation of 1974, discussed earlier, revealed that whereas that the goals of the recommendation had been included in the curriculum to a great extent, the same is not true with respect to teacher education programs (UNESCO 2018).

6.1 Standards

Education is an intentional, goal-oriented process. Teachers work in institutions which are normed by a shared commitment to achieve certain goals and standards. Using standards as a lever for educational change is a common and effective strategy to reform education systems. If we want teachers to educate their students to be globally competent, this should be included in the standards. Very often it is not. As standards incorporate global education, choices need to be made about what to cover and how. Because education for sustainable development and global citizenship is one of the targets of the UN Sustainable Development Goals focused on education, that target and the proposed indicators are a useful place to start in any education system:

> Target 4.7. Sustainable development and global citizenship. By 2030, ensure that all learners acquire the knowledge and skills needed to promote sustainable development, including, among others, through education for sustainable development and sustainable lifestyles, human rights, gender equality, promotion of a culture of peace and non-violence, global citizenship and appreciation of cultural diversity and of culture's contribution to sustainable development.
>
> Global Indicator 4.7.1—Extent to which (i) global citizenship education and (ii) education for sustainable development, including gender equality and human rights, are mainstreamed at all levels in (a) national education policies, (b) curricula, (c) teacher education, and (d) student assessment.
>
> Thematic indicator 26—Percentage of students by age group (or education level) showing adequate understanding of issues relating to global citizenship and sustainability.
>
> Thematic indicator 27—Percentage of 15-year-old students showing proficiency in knowledge of environmental science and geoscience.
>
> Thematic indicator 28—Percentage of schools that provide life skills-based HIV and sexuality education
>
> Thematic indicator 29—Extent to which the framework on the World Programme on Human Rights Education is implemented nationally (as per UNGA Resolution 59/113) (United Nations 2020).

Underscoring the importance of addressing global education in standards in the United States, in a study of social studies teaching in Indiana, teachers reported that they would pay more attention to global citizenship education if it was included in the Indiana Academic Social Studies Standards (Rapoport 2010, p. 185).

A number of countries which have a national curriculum and national standards have included global education. Australia adopted a national curriculum only in 2009, which gives prominent attention to global education, a topic which received high priority in the ministerial Melbourne Declaration on Educational Goals for Young Australian, which "established Global Citizenship Education as a key goal for Australian schooling…In stating this aim there is a clear intention that young Australians not only understand global issues, but come to see themselves as participating citizens within their local, national and global communities" (Peterson et al. 2018, p. 7). The Australian curriculum includes three cross-curriculum priorities, focusing on Aboriginal Cultures, Asia and engagement with Asia and Sustainability

6.1 Standards

(Australian Curriculum 2019). The Department of Education sees the entire Australian Curriculum as a Global Education Curriculum, and has developed a series of resources to insert global education in the curriculum (Commonwealth of Australia 2012). In spite of the fact that the curriculum makes global citizenship education a priority, it does not define it, leaving it up to schools to develop specific curriculum. This accounts for great heterogeneity across schools in terms of what global education looks like in practice (Peterson et al. 2018).

Once standards incorporate global education, they may cover a variety of themes, reflecting the various definitions and intellectual traditions of global education mentioned earlier. For instance, a comparison of social studies curricula in developed and developing countries found differences in how the process of globalization was covered. Whereas standards in US social studies courses emphasize globalization primarily as an economic process, in developing countries this process was covered more multidimensionally (Beltramo and Duncheon 2013). A study of two programs of global education in the United States also concludes that social studies standards do not adequately include the study of the process of globalization or the study of human rights. In 2000, only twenty US states included human rights education in their curriculum (Myers 2006).

As an effort to provide states with frameworks they could include in their standards, the US Council of Chief State School Officers, in partnership with the Asia Society, developed a matrix which provides guidance on what students should be able to do to demonstrate global competency. This matrix defines Global Competence as "the capacity and disposition to understand and act on issues of global significance" (Boix et al. 2011). This capacity encompasses four skills: investigate the world, recognize perspectives, communicate ideas and take action. For each of these, it provides four specific definitions of what students should be able to demonstrate. The Asia Society has further developed performance outcomes and rubrics for global competence in the context of the subjects of mathematics, science, language, history and social studies, and arts (Asia Society 2019).

In the United States, various states have included global education in their standards. For example, in North Carolina the State Board appointed a task force of global education which developed a strategy, including dual language immersion programs, the designation of global-ready schools, and a global education badge for students (North Carolina State Board for Education 2013). The State Board also developed a global education rubric, designed to support schools as they developed their own global education curriculum and recommended that districts "provide content for embedding global themes and problem-based learning that focuses on global issues, including history, social studies and geography, throughout the K-12 curriculum consistent with the Common Core State Standards, the North Carolina Essential Standards, and the NC Professional Teaching Standards, including guidelines specific to a global-ready designated graduation Project" (North Carolina Department of Public Instruction 2017).

The United States Department of Education has produced a framework for "Developing Global and Cultural Competencies to Advance Equity, Excellence and Economic Competitiveness" which proposes standards for early learning, elementary, secondary and college, as well as for collaboration and communication, world languages, diverse perspective, and civic and global engagement.

The overarching goals of the framework are to educate globally and culturally competent individuals who are:

> Proficient in at least two languages; Aware of differences that exist between cultures, open to diverse perspectives, and appreciative of insight gained through open cultural exchange; Critical and creative thinkers, who can apply understanding of diverse cultures, beliefs, economies, technology and forms of government in order to work effectively in cross-cultural settings to address societal, environmental or entrepreneurial challenges; Able to operate at a professional level in intercultural and international contexts and to continue to develop new skills and harness technology to support continued growth. (US Department of Education 2017)

Obviously, national standards and curriculum need not explicitly use the term "global education" to include goals which are global in nature. For instance, world languages, geography or world history, or science, or covering themes such as universal human rights, appreciation for diversity, peace, climate change or pandemics, are all avenues to develop global competencies.

For instance, in the United States, the new science standards, a set of standards for voluntary adoption by States developed by the National Research Council, the National Science Foundation, the American Association for the Advancement of Science and the National Science Teacher Association, have introduced the subject of climate change in elementary school, with opportunities for deeper study in middle and high school (Chen 2017).

Standards can also include teacher preparation. For example, various states in the United States have included dimensions related to global education in their teacher preparation standards. North Carolina, for instance, included "global awareness" in its teacher standards.

6.2 Curriculum and Pedagogy

Students can access opportunities to develop global competency through a variety of curricula: infused within the existing disciplines, in a separate course in the curriculum, as part of travel abroad, and in extra-curricular activities. There are some subjects that are squarely focused on global competency, such as foreign languages, geography, and world history. Specialized courses can be also made available focusing explicitly on global themes, such as AP Development Economics or AP Human Geography or World History. Students can also participate in projects which provide them an opportunity to study global themes, such as research projects in various courses. Student clubs or travel abroad can also augment opportunities for students to develop global competency. The World Course proposed a dedicated space in the curriculum focused exclusively on the development of global competencies because we thought of this course as a structure that would support the integration of knowledge from different disciplines on behalf of learning to think and act about global topics and challenges. These two options—integrating global education in the curriculum versus personalized opportunities—are not mutually excluding, but complementary. An important question in designing curriculum is how to balance offering opportunity to students who are interested in global education with ensuring all students acquire a minimum baseline of knowledge. The skills and knowledge required in a traditional curriculum—language, math, sciences—are not optional, but essential requirements to participate in society. The same is true for global competency. Why should religious literacy, understanding of climate dynamics, or cross-cultural awareness be optional in a world increasingly interdependent? Richard Haass, President of the Council of Foreign Relations in the United States, in a recent book on global themes states, "A search of graduation requirements at most American institutions of higher learning reveals it is possible to graduate from nearly any two or four year college or university in the United States, be it a community college or an Ivy League institution, without gaining even a rudimentary understanding of the world" (Haass 2020, xv).

The late professor Hans Rosling undertook the measurement of the basic knowledge of facts about the world among people in various countries. The levels of knowledge he found were so abysmally low that he dubbed his project "the ignorance survey." In the United States, for example, adults had very low levels of knowledge about the world population. In a three-item response question, only 7% correctly answered predictions regarding the expected total number of people in 2100, 29% knew in which continent most people lived, 53% knew current life expectancy of the world population, 22% knew current literacy levels, 25% knew world income distribution, 24% knew average level of schooling of the population, 17% knew the percentage of the population vaccinated against measles, 5% knew changes in poverty rates over the last decade, 46% knew what percentage of world energy comes from solar and wind power, and 45% knew global fertility rates (Gapminder 2013).

Even though there are many curriculum resources available, there is still much to be done to include global education content in national curricula around the world. The World Program on Human Rights Education of the United Nations High Commissioner for Human Rights developed curricula to teach human rights. The program proposed integrating human rights education in primary and secondary schools. An evaluation conducted in 2010 revealed that most of the respondents had integrated human rights education into national curricula and standards, mostly as a cross-curricular issue, usually in civics or social studies classes. (UNESCO 2017, p. 290). A study conducted by UNESCO and the Georg Eckert Institute for International Textbook Research revealed that the study of the Holocaust was included in the curriculum in about half of the 135 countries surveyed, usually relating it to local histories of human rights violations (UNESCO 2017, p. 290). Coverage of sexual and reproductive health issues are unevenly addressed in curricula around the world (Ibid).

A recent UNESCO report examined curriculum frameworks in 78 countries between 2005 and 2015 in terms of target 4.7 of the UN Sustainable Development Goals. The topics most commonly addressed include rights (88%) and democracy

(79%) and some emphasis on sustainable development in three-quarters of the countries. Less commonly addressed are terms related to global citizenship: only half mention multiculturalism and interculturalism and 10% mention global inequality. Less than 15% of the countries address gender equality (UNESCO 2017, p. 292).

Several organizations have proposed pedagogies to support global education. For instance, the OECD and the Asia Society developed a resource guide which discusses the value of several instructional approaches to develop global competency, including structured debates, organized discussions, current events discussions, playing games, project-based learning and service-learning, and provides multiple examples of what effective global education practices look like (OECD and Asia Society 2018, p. 6).

Drawing on empirical research and analysis of good practice, the Alberta Council for Environmental Education (2017) identifies six key principles of excellent climate change education:

(i) Frame climate change education in ways that focus on solutions, rather than on problems, build a positive narrative around shared identity. Focus on energy, conservation, and outdoors education. Rely on pedagogies which engage in deliberative discussions, promote exchanges with scientists, address misconceptions, and implement school and community projects.
(ii) Keep the audience in mind. Develop curriculum that is appropriate to the age of the child, support teachers.
(iii) Design programs which are action-oriented. Build agency of students.
(iv) Develop activities that extend beyond climate science, including imagining a positive desired future, focus on local content, teach students how to think, not what to think, do not scare students.
(v) Establish connections to the curriculum and identify competencies. Emphasize cross-curricular approaches, cultivate systems thinking, and help students understand the interdependencies between climate change mitigation, adaptation, and resilience.
(vi) Evaluate for program improvement.

An empirical study of teaching practices for global readiness identified four factors as important: (1) Situated practice, so that learning is contextual and relevant to the students; (2) integrated global learning, teachers demonstrate the connections between local and global events; (3) critical literacy, teachers provide texts about past and present international events from multiple perspectives; (4) transactional experiences, students engage in intercultural-dialogue (Kerkhoff 2017, pp. 102–103). These four factors include the following items:

Situated Practice

> I take inventory of the cultures represented by my students
> I cultivate a classroom environment that values diversity
> I cultivate a classroom environment that promotes equality
> I provide a space that allows learners to take risks
> I provide a space that allows students a voice
> I attempt to break down students' stereotypes

Integrated Global Learning

    I integrate global learning with the existing curriculum
    I build a repertoire of resources related to global education
    I use inquiry-based lessons about the world
    I assess students' global learning

Critical Literacy Instruction

    I ask students to engage in discussions about international current events
    I ask students to analyze the reliability of a source
    I ask students to analyze content from multiple perspectives
    I ask students to analyze the agenda behind media messages
    I ask students to construct claims based on primary sources

Transactional experiences

    I bring in speakers from different backgrounds so students can listen to different experiences
    I ask students to utilize synchronous technology for international collaborations
    I ask students to utilize asynchronous technology for international collaboration
    I ask students to utilize technology for virtual interviews (Kerkhoff 2017, p. 103)

A study of three groups of social studies teachers, with varying levels of expertise, identified a number of shared pedagogical practices across the three groups. They connected global content to students' lives, included students' cultural backgrounds in the curriculum, and established connections across geographies and historical periods. In addition, exemplary teachers explicitly examined the relationship between local and global inequality, created opportunities for cross-cultural learning, organized global curriculum around themes, issues or problems, emphasized higher-order thinking and research skills, and deployed a variety of pedagogical strategies (Merryfield 1998).

A case study of the pedagogies used by an elementary school teacher identified the following "signature pedagogies" for global education: clear global purpose, disciplinary foundation, integrative units, spiraling repeated presence in the curriculum, meeting student's needs, and openness to teacher inquiry (Boix Mansilla 2013).

Based on these findings, another study examined the global education pedagogies used by ten teachers in North Carolina in various subjects. "The three signature pedagogies evident across content areas were: (1) intentional integration of global topics and multiple perspectives into and across the standard curriculum; (2) ongoing authentic engagement with global issues; and (3) connecting teachers' global experiences, students' global experiences, and the curriculum" (Tichnor-Wagner et al. 2016, p. 12).

Foreign language instruction is an integral part of global education, and there is well-established knowledge about which approaches are most effective. For instance, dual language immersion is a very productive approach to educating coordinated speakers of two languages. One of the clearly established principles is that foreign language proficiency requires time, years of study, and access to courses at various levels of proficiency. Many schools offer only introductory level courses and devote too limited time to allow students to gain foreign language proficiency. The Modern Language Association is an excellent resource to provide access to curriculum, pedagogies and assessment resources in foreign languages (Modern Language Association 2019). It is possible to adopt these principles in designing effective and rigorous foreign language programs in public schools. The State of Utah has adopted an ambitious program of dual language immersion offering five modern languages (Chinese, French, German, Portuguese, or Spanish) through a program that brings teachers who are native speakers of those languages to Utah (Utah State Board of Education 2019).

Other pedagogies for global education involve engaging students in study abroad. Global education programs can engage students in service projects or problem-based projects of the sort we included in the World Course. It is typical of many global education pedagogies to seek to cultivate the agency of students, engaging them with real problems and in processes where they attempt to generate solutions to those problems. These activities often involve working in groups, and working on challenges which may not have an obvious solution and where part of the learning opportunity is figuring out how to frame the problem. The value of these skills for life and work is clear, as the challenges adults face seldom come structured in a way that has an obvious solution or much scaffolding to solve them. These concerns were central in the design of the World Course:

> In addition, rather than imposing on the students a list of the discrete skills, knowledge, and attitudes that we wished to impart to them, we wanted the students to find and make meaning in their learning. Thus, the World Course curriculum focuses on learning that is integrated and grounded in current social, political, economic, and other concerns and specifically on issues that are complex and without easy answers or solutions. We believed that students would find value in—and would desire to engage with—issues that are "real" and authentic; similarly, we believed that in being asked to engage with these real-life issues, the learners would be more motivated to learn the skills and knowledge necessary to understand and solve these issues. For example, the curriculum centers on issues like immigration and the impact of human migration on the environment and on the kinds of knowledge, skills, and attitudes that are necessary to address these issues. That approach led us to fields such as demography, which is not a subject taught in many schools but is a topic that we thought was essential for learning how to address issues about population growth and its impact on sustainability. (Reimers et al. 2016)

Recent studies show that there are opportunities to improve pedagogies around the world to bring them in line with current science-based evidence on how to support deeper learning and twenty-first-century skills. In a study of teaching and teaching practices conducted by the OECD, pedagogies that require cognitive activation or that rely on enhanced activities are less frequently used than pedagogies focused on classroom management or teacher-directed instruction, as shown in Table 6.1.

The same study shows that, on average, among the 48 countries participating in the study, only two in five teachers in lower secondary schools report that they present their students with tasks for which there is no obvious solution, only three in five give students tasks that require them to think critically, only half ask students

6.2 Curriculum and Pedagogy

Table 6.1 Teaching practices. *Percentage of lower secondary teachers who "frequently" or "always" use the following practices in their class[1] (OECD average-31)*

	OECD average-31	Percentage of teachers who "frequently" or "always" use the following practices in their class (%)
Classroom management	Tell students to follow classroom rules	70.7
	Tell students to listen to what I say	70.2
	Calm students who are disruptive	65.0
	When the lesson begins, tell students to quieten down quickly	61.1
Clarity of instruction	Explain what I expect students to learn	89.9
	Explain how new and old topics are related	83.9
	Set goals at the beginning of instruction	80.5
	Refer to a problem from everyday life or work to demonstrate why new knowledge is useful	73.7
	Present a summary of recently learned content	73.5
	Let students practice similar tasks until I know that every student has understood the subject matter	67.9
Cognitive activation	Give tasks that require students to think critically	58.1
	Have students work in small groups to come up with a joint solution to a problem or task	50.1
	Ask students to decide on their own procedures for solving complex tasks	44.5
	Present tasks for which there is no obvious solution	33.9
Enhanced activities	Let students use ICT for projects or classwork	52.7
	Give students projects that require at least one week to complete	28.6

Source OECD (2019a, Fig. I.2.1)

to decide on their own how to solve complex tasks, only half have students work in small groups to solve a problem, and less than a third ask students to work on projects which require at least a week to complete. Additionally, only half of the teachers allow students to use ICT to work on projects or classwork. These are all opportunities that would help students develop important twenty-first-century skills, and they could all be readily deployed in global education projects. For instance, all of these activities are commonly used throughout the World Course (OECD 2019a) (Table 6.2).

Learning is a social activity, students learn not only from their teachers, but also from their peers, as they interact with them. This is a reason promoting interaction and collaboration among students of different backgrounds and identities can not only help reduce prejudice and stereotyping, but also develop essential skills to collaborate with others in diverse societies. An obvious implication of this is the value of structuring diverse classrooms and schools that are as inclusive and diverse as possible so that students have opportunities to interact with and learn from peers who are different. A diverse classroom and school will help students not only experience the benefits of learning from and with peers who are different, it will also help them articulate this experience with the academic study of concepts such as "human rights." These benefits of inclusion are reflected in UNESCO's (1994) Salamanca Statement on Principles, Policies and Practice in Special Needs Education, recommending the inclusion of all types of learners in the same educational environment, as inclusive schools and classrooms are most effective in "combating discriminatory attitudes, creating welcoming environments, building an inclusive society and achieving education for all" (UNESCO 1994, para 2). Schools that systematically exclude or discriminate against students with particular identities, such as students with special learning needs or nonbinary gender identities, teach a powerful lesson in bigotry to students about what is acceptable that will undermine any academic emphasis on the study of universal human rights in the curriculum. A recent World Bank report documents that children and youth with disabilities, indigenous identities and sexual and gender minorities are the most excluded and discriminated against in schools around the world (World Bank 2019).

Another means to provide students opportunities to collaborate with diverse peers is to offer them opportunities to travel abroad or to collaborate with peers in other countries using technology, as a way to expand the range of opportunities to benefit from collaborations with diverse peers beyond the diversity reflected in the composition of their schools. Building school-to-school partnerships requires thoughtful design so that it provides all students an opportunity to learn and not simply reinforce prejudice or a mindset that some students are "saviors" who can do for other communities what they cannot do for themselves (Klein 2017).

Yet, structuring schools that are racially, religiously, or socioeconomically diverse, or engaging students in collaborations with peers in other countries, is not enough to provide students with opportunities that are formative and beneficial to all. As cited earlier, Allport, in his pioneering work on racial prejudice, outlined conditions for positive inter-racial interactions as including equal status, cooperation, common goals and support from authorities. Results from the OECD study of teachers show

6.2 Curriculum and Pedagogy

Table 6.2 Teaching practices. *Results based on responses of lower secondary teachers*

	Present tasks for which there is no obvious solution (%)	Give tasks that require students to think critically (%)	Have students work in small groups to come up with a joint solution to a problem or task (%)	Ask students to decide on their own procedures for solving complex tasks (%)	Refer to a problem from everyday life or work to demonstrate why new knowledge is useful (%)	Give students projects that require at least one week to complete (%)	Let students use ICT2 for projects or classwork (%)
Alberta (Canada)	31.8	76.0	56.7	54.9	74.6	44.0	65.7
Australia	29.2	69.5	51.3	44.1	72.1	46.2	78.2
Austria	12.4	47.2	42.5	35.5	74.8	17.0	32.9
Belgium	30.9	43.7	34.1	25.0	68.4	21.5	28.9
– Flemish Comm. (*Belgium*)	25.3	39.9	41.6	27.2	73.9	21.8	37.8
Brazil	48.9	84.2	55.6	39.5	91.3	43.4	41.6
Bulgaria	19.7	60.6	48.6	52.5	81.9	36.9	44.2
CABA (Argentina)	60.3	81.3	70.7	57.7	74.8	52.4	64.0
Chile	57.7	70.0	71.0	67.1	88.2	50.8	63.4
Colombia	61.9	87.5	85.0	65.3	92.0	55.2	70.8
Croatia	34.2	60.4	30.7	22.3	90.1	13.0	46.2
Cyprus	32.2	75.0	52.1	46.5	82.5	25.6	54.2
Czech Republic	10.6	39.8	27.3	32.7	69.2	8.7	35.4
Denmark	50.8	61.1	80.3	51.8	60.9	24.9	90.4
England (UK)	33.6	67.5	50.9	43.4	65.2	31.3	41.3
Estonia	16.4	46.2	39.5	29.0	68.2	14.4	45.6
Finland	34.5	37.2	42.3	26.3	68.2	22.4	50.7

(continued)

Table 6.2 (continued)

	Present tasks for which there is no obvious solution (%)	Give tasks that require students to think critically (%)	Have students work in small groups to come up with a joint solution to a problem or task (%)	Ask students to decide on their own procedures for solving complex tasks (%)	Refer to a problem from everyday life or work to demonstrate why new knowledge is useful (%)	Give students projects that require at least one week to complete (%)	Let students use ICT2 for projects or classwork (%)
France	25.9	50.3	49.2	26.3	57.5	27.4	36.1
Georgia	48.1	76.8	62.4	67.9	74.4	25.8	53.3
Hungary	28.3	55.9	35.5	36.3	84.7	9.9	48.1
Iceland	19.4	50.1	44.5	52.6	40.5	30.8	54.0
Israel	34.2	48.6	35.0	35.4	71.2	28.4	51.8
Italy	44.2	67.7	45.7	43.3	82.5	20.2	46.6
Japan	16.1	12.6	44.4	24.9	53.9	11.1	17.9
Kazakhstan	61.4	78.6	79.3	75.4	82.4	33.6	65.7
Korea	38.1	44.8	59.2	50.8	82.1	31.4	29.6
Latvia	57.4	73.4	46.7	45.5	88.5	21.3	48.3
Lithuania	13.4	76.6	52.2	69.1	87.1	25.6	61.8
Malta	30.9	59.6	42.7	40.6	77.3	35.3	48.0
Mexico	38.4	67.4	70.9	67.6	89.2	53.8	68.7
Netherlands	39.4	54.3	47.7	39.9	64.2	27.7	51.3
New Zealand	28.7	69.4	59.5	50.9	72.6	42.3	79.8
Norway	53.1	51.1	63.0	52.5	66.5	28.8	m
Portugal	67.3	68.4	49.9	44.5	93.1	32.2	56.8
Romania	22.3	67.9	52.8	43.7	83.1	33.7	56.2
Russia	58.1	59.7	42.5	44.9	79.5	25.9	69.0

(continued)

6.2 Curriculum and Pedagogy

Table 6.2 (continued)

	Present tasks for which there is no obvious solution (%)	Give tasks that require students to think critically (%)	Have students work in small groups to come up with a joint solution to a problem or task (%)	Ask students to decide on their own procedures for solving complex tasks (%)	Refer to a problem from everyday life or work to demonstrate why new knowledge is useful (%)	Give students projects that require at least one week to complete (%)	Let students use ICT2 for projects or classwork (%)
Saudi Arabia	43.9	62.2	72.4	55.8	77.8	42.1	48.6
Shanghai (China)	43.7	53.3	70.0	67.4	91.7	20.8	24.3
Singapore	35.3	54.1	44.9	36.3	70.9	34.3	42.8
Slovak Republic	29.9	59.1	40.2	48.7	72.0	15.8	47.3
Slovenia	29.5	57.6	28.4	28.3	80.1	11.6	36.5
South Africa	52.3	83.1	54.1	53.9	83.5	55.8	38.3
Spain	44.2	65.4	45.9	41.1	81.2	33.0	51.4
Sweden	24.7	48.9	51.5	44.6	58.6	34.9	63.3
Chinese Taipei	36.4	48.8	40.2	39.3	84.3	20.3	14.7
Turkey	21.9	54.7	43.9	57.1	86.6	30.2	66.6
United Arab Emirates	46.7	82.4	84.2	70.0	85.0	54.7	76.8
United States	27.6	78.9	59.7	45.9	71.3	33.0	60.1
Vietnam	73.7	41.3	73.6	60.2	87.2	24.7	42.8
OECD average-31	33.9	58.1	50.1	44.5	73.7	28.6	52.7
EU total-23	34.1	60.0	46.7	39.1	73.1	26.1	46.1
TALIS average-48	37.5	61.0	52.7	47.0	76.7	30.5	51.3

Source OECD (2019a, Table I.2.1)

the potential of diverse classrooms to support the development of global education curriculum as many teachers work in ethnically diverse classrooms, support activities or organizations encouraging expression of such diversity, organize multicultural events, teach students how to deal with ethnic and cultural discrimination, and adopt teaching and learning practices that integrate global education, as shown in Table 6.3. At the same time, the table shows that not all teachers adopt these practices, underscoring the importance of professional development to intentionally deploy classroom diversity in service of global education. On average, among the 47 countries participating in the study, 63% of the teachers support activities or organizations encouraging students' expressions of diverse ethnic and cultural identities, 54% organize multicultural events, 73% teach students how to deal with cultural and ethnic discrimination, and 83% adopt teaching and learning practices that integrate global issues across the curriculum.

A considerable number of teachers reports that they experience challenges teaching in culturally diverse classrooms. On average, for all countries in the OECD, 67% of teachers report that they can cope with the challenges of a multicultural classroom; 59% say that they can adapt their teaching to the cultural diversity of their students; 69% say they can make students with an immigrant background work with others who don't share the same background; 68% say they can raise awareness about cultural differences; and 73% say they can reduce ethnic stereotyping among students (OECD 2019a, Table I.3.38) (Table 6.4).

The OECD report on teachers identifies professional development to work with the growing diversity of classrooms as a priority:

> Not many teachers are trained in teaching in such culturally or linguistically diverse classrooms. Thirty-five percent of teachers report that teaching in multicultural and multilingual settings was included in their formal teacher education or training, and 22% of teachers said it was included in their professional development activities in the 12 months prior to the survey. Furthermore, teachers who have previously taught in a classroom with students from different cultures report that they do not all feel confident in their ability to cater to the needs of diverse classrooms. When teachers completed their formal teacher education or training, only 26% of them felt well or very well prepared for teaching in a multicultural or multilingual setting. At the time of survey completion, 33% of teachers still do not feel able to cope with the challenges of a multicultural classroom, on average across the OECD. Teaching in a multicultural or multilingual setting is one of the professional development activities with the highest proportion of teachers reporting a high need for it (15%). While a high percentage of teachers (almost 70%) report high levels of self-efficacy with respect to promoting positive relationships and interactions between students from different backgrounds, fewer teachers (59%) feel able to adapt their teaching to the cultural diversity of students. (OECD 2019a, p. 31).

Table 6.5 presents the percentage of teachers who identify a need for professional development in teaching in multicultural settings, teaching cross-curricular skills or working with people from different cultures.

It is particularly important to ensure that the growing diversity of schools and classrooms indeed translates into positive opportunities for all students. There is some evidence that minority students experience discrimination and bullying in schools.

6.2 Curriculum and Pedagogy

Table 6.3 School practices related to diversity. *Results based on responses of lower secondary teachers and principals*

Percentage of teachers working in a school with diverse ethnic and cultural student background[1] where the following diversity-related practices are implemented

	Supporting activities or organizations encouraging students' expression of diverse ethnic and cultural identities				Organizing multicultural events				Teaching how to deal with ethnic and cultural discrimination				Adopting teaching and learning practices that integrate global issues throughout the curriculum			
	According to teachers		According to principals[2]		According to teachers		According to principals[2]		According to teachers		According to principals[2]		According to teachers		According to principals[2]	
	%	S.E.	%	S.E.	%	S.E.	%	S.E.	%	S.E.	%	S.E.	%	S.E.	%	S.E.
Alberta (Canada)	75.2	(2.2)	83.9	(5.0)	58.3	(3.3)	59.4	(4.8)	78.3	(1.6)	81.9	(3.8)	87.6	(1.1)	90.1	(4.0)
Austria	50.6	(1.5)	64.8	(3.5)	39.1	(2.3)	51.3	(4.0)	75.6	(1.2)	83.6	(2.9)	87.9	(0.8)	95.0	(1.2)
Belgium	52.1	(1.3)	59.3	(3.1)	51.6	(1.6)	57.7	(3.5)	75.8	(0.9)	85.5	(2.4)	60.6	(1.0)	78.0	(2.5)
– Flemish Comm. (Belgium)	47.5	(1.7)	48.6	(4.3)	57.4	(2.3)	62.3	(4.3)	74.6	(1.1)	86.6	(2.9)	63.5	(1.3)	78.3	(3.7)
Brazil	76.8	(1.9)	85.9	(3.4)	82.1	(1.9)	90.4	(2.9)	80.5	(1.9)	92.1	(2.5)	85.6	(1.8)	99.4	(0.6)
Bulgaria	73.3	(1.7)	80.7	(3.1)	63.4	(1.8)	73.4	(3.2)	62.9	(1.5)	71.2	(3.6)	69.2	(1.5)	79.6	(3.2)
CABA (Argentina)	73.1	(1.8)	73.2	(5.6)	67.1	(2.5)	68.0	(6.4)	90.0	(1.6)	95.3	(2.2)	81.1	(1.4)	94.7	(2.1)
Chile	76.6	(1.8)	88.0	(2.3)	67.7	(2.5)	81.8	(3.2)	85.3	(1.1)	90.9	(3.0)	75.8	(1.6)	90.2	(2.9)
Colombia	81.5	(2.7)	88.8	(4.5)	79.0	(3.7)	86.7	(4.0)	88.2	(3.6)	81.1	(8.9)	84.8	(2.4)	88.6	(4.5)
Croatia	49.2	(2.2)	59.4	(5.2)	36.0	(2.7)	46.1	(5.2)	69.2	(1.7)	77.3	(4.6)	62.4	(1.7)	71.1	(4.0)
Cyprus	74.1	(1.8)	84.5	(4.2)	60.9	(2.2)	78.2	(5.1)	67.3	(2.0)	79.1	(5.3)	64.1	(1.8)	81.7	(4.7)
Czech Republic	38.0	(1.7)	49.5	(4.5)	29.6	(2.1)	40.9	(4.6)	69.6	(1.4)	81.5	(4.0)	75.8	(1.3)	86.5	(3.1)
Denmark	22.8	(1.6)	23.6	(3.9)	16.9	(2.0)	17.3	(3.9)	26.1	(1.9)	26.5	(4.3)	54.1	(1.8)	70.2	(4.4)

(continued)

Table 6.3 (continued)

	Percentage of teachers working in a school with diverse ethnic and cultural student background[1] where the following diversity-related practices are implemented															
	Supporting activities or organizations encouraging students' expression of diverse ethnic and cultural identities				Organizing multicultural events				Teaching how to deal with ethnic and cultural discrimination				Adopting teaching and learning practices that integrate global issues throughout the curriculum			
	According to teachers		According to principals[2]		According to teachers		According to principals[2]		According to teachers		According to principals[2]		According to teachers		According to principals[2]	
	%	S.E.	%	S.E.	%	S.E.	%	S.E.	%	S.E.	%	S.E.	%	S.E.	%	S.E.
England (UK)	69.3	(1.4)	89.7	(2.7)	51.4	(2.0)	68.9	(4.0)	84.1	(1.1)	94.5	(2.0)	80.3	(1.0)	91.3	(2.4)
Estonia	69.7	(2.1)	72.5	(5.8)	59.4	(3.1)	67.9	(5.0)	65.2	(1.8)	72.2	(6.1)	73.7	(1.7)	68.3	(5.3)
Finland	29.7	(1.6)	35.5	(4.7)	38.6	(2.4)	51.0	(4.9)	72.5	(1.2)	84.1	(3.7)	76.5	(1.2)	94.2	(2.1)
France	53.4	(1.8)	55.2	(4.4)	32.2	(2.1)	45.6	(4.4)	79.5	(1.1)	86.1	(3.1)	71.8	(1.3)	78.5	(3.2)
Georgia	72.5	(2.0)	82.3	(4.6)	66.6	(1.9)	80.0	(4.4)	81.6	(1.7)	94.4	(2.3)	80.9	(1.5)	83.1	(5.1)
Hungary	50.5	(2.1)	53.7	(4.9)	40.9	(2.8)	46.6	(4.5)	64.4	(1.7)	74.6	(4.3)	60.8	(1.5)	60.6	(4.5)
Iceland	49.8	(1.8)	48.4	(0.5)	35.6	(1.7)	43.6	(0.6)	54.5	(1.9)	76.7	(0.5)	27.2	(1.6)	37.6	(0.5)
Israel	60.2	(2.2)	67.2	(6.5)	74.2	(1.7)	85.3	(5.2)	66.1	(1.5)	80.1	(5.3)	54.7	(1.3)	64.7	(5.9)
Italy	57.5	(1.5)	67.8	(4.2)	33.9	(2.0)	49.6	(4.1)	67.1	(1.3)	67.1	(3.6)	76.4	(1.1)	86.0	(3.0)
Japan	28.5	(2.5)	25.0	(4.5)	30.1	(3.1)	32.4	(5.2)	51.9	(2.2)	73.6	(4.5)	37.7	(2.2)	51.9	(5.4)
Kazakhstan	86.9	(1.1)	93.3	(2.2)	92.6	(0.8)	93.7	(2.4)	83.2	(1.3)	88.0	(2.8)	69.4	(1.2)	77.5	(3.6)

(continued)

6.2 Curriculum and Pedagogy 93

Table 6.3 (continued)

	Percentage of teachers working in a school with diverse ethnic and cultural student background[1] where the following diversity-related practices are implemented															
	Supporting activities or organizations encouraging students' expression of diverse ethnic and cultural identities				Organizing multicultural events				Teaching how to deal with ethnic and cultural discrimination				Adopting teaching and learning practices that integrate global issues throughout the curriculum			
	According to teachers		According to principals[2]		According to teachers		According to principals[2]		According to teachers		According to principals[2]		According to teachers		According to principals[2]	
	%	S.E.	%	S.E.	%	S.E.	%	S.E.	%	S.E.	%	S.E.	%	S.E.	%	S.E.
Korea	48.0	(2.4)	61.2	(6.3)	43.1	(3.3)	54.2	(7.1)	73.4	(1.8)	89.8	(4.2)	43.2	(2.0)	71.3	(5.7)
Latvia	59.0	(2.1)	49.2	(6.5)	58.3	(2.5)	68.1	(6.0)	73.7	(1.9)	82.6	(4.5)	76.8	(1.3)	89.8	(3.2)
Lithuania	65.9	(2.5)	80.3	(6.1)	72.7	(3.0)	91.1	(3.1)	75.5	(2.1)	89.3	(3.8)	69.5	(1.9)	77.9	(5.6)
Malta	73.5	(2.8)	92.6	(4.8)	59.0	(5.0)	88.3	(6.6)	69.7	(1.3)	98.0	(1.2)	71.4	(1.4)	91.1	(4.6)
Mexico	66.8	(5.1)	66.2	(8.6)	46.1	(5.4)	50.9	(9.6)	83.5	(2.7)	82.5	(6.7)	74.6	(2.8)	86.7	(6.4)
Netherlands	42.5	(2.0)	40.3	(7.0)	28.9	(3.7)	32.2	(6.8)	68.0	(2.2)	83.5	(4.6)	51.2	(1.6)	72.4	(6.7)
New Zealand	97.6	(0.5)	99.7	(0.3)	82.5	(1.8)	88.7	(2.5)	66.6	(1.6)	73.2	(3.8)	84.7	(1.1)	94.4	(1.9)
Norway	22.7	(0.9)	15.6	(3.1)	19.5	(1.5)	21.8	(3.5)	56.8	(1.2)	60.7	(4.4)	77.6	(0.9)	88.2	(2.9)
Portugal	52.0	(1.3)	66.6	(4.3)	43.0	(1.7)	51.2	(4.1)	78.4	(1.0)	91.7	(2.2)	73.5	(1.1)	92.6	(2.2)
Romania	76.9	(1.5)	96.0	(1.7)	69.4	(1.5)	87.5	(2.9)	82.5	(1.2)	92.6	(2.2)	76.0	(1.4)	84.3	(3.6)
Russia	68.2	(2.2)	80.9	(3.5)	64.3	(2.6)	82.0	(4.6)	75.6	(1.1)	83.5	(4.6)	57.3	(1.6)	49.8	(5.1)

(continued)

Table 6.3 (continued)

	Percentage of teachers working in a school with diverse ethnic and cultural student background[1] where the following diversity-related practices are implemented															
	Supporting activities or organizations encouraging students' expression of diverse ethnic and cultural identities				Organizing multicultural events				Teaching how to deal with ethnic and cultural discrimination				Adopting teaching and learning practices that integrate global issues throughout the curriculum			
	According to teachers		According to principals[2]		According to teachers		According to principals[2]		According to teachers		According to principals[2]		According to teachers		According to principals[2]	
	%	S.E.	%	S.E.	%	S.E.	%	S.E.	%	S.E.	%	S.E.	%	S.E.	%	S.E.
Saudi Arabia	65.6	(3.0)	63.0	(7.9)	49.7	(3.1)	47.0	(7.1)	63.8	(2.8)	63.7	(8.0)	48.3	(2.9)	45.6	(7.7)
Shanghai (China)	90.7	(1.2)	95.4	(2.2)	88.3	(1.4)	97.5	(1.6)	79.9	(1.8)	94.9	(2.4)	74.4	(2.1)	71.8	(5.2)
Singapore	92.5	(0.5)	98.0	(0.1)	94.7	(0.4)	99.1	(0.1)	87.0	(0.7)	95.4	(0.1)	88.4	(0.6)	93.8	(0.1)
Slovak Republic	58.7	(1.5)	69.7	(1.0)	39.9	(1.5)	58.8	(1.0)	72.0	(1.5)	85.2	(0.9)	70.6	(1.4)	80.1	(0.8)
Slovenia	43.6	(2.5)	69.6	(5.6)	41.5	(3.3)	48.7	(6.0)	86.9	(1.1)	92.5	(2.9)	65.6	(1.6)	76.2	(4.9)
South Africa	83.7	(1.4)	83.9	(4.1)	73.8	(2.1)	75.2	(4.7)	80.6	(1.9)	82.9	(4.3)	82.7	(1.3)	84.7	(4.0)
Spain	64.1	(1.5)	75.7	(3.1)	45.7	(1.4)	56.3	(3.5)	77.9	(0.9)	86.4	(2.6)	72.4	(0.8)	90.7	(2.2)
Sweden	26.7	(1.2)	32.1	(0.5)	25.3	(1.1)	35.8	(0.5)	69.6	(1.2)	81.2	(0.4)	77.9	(1.4)	93.1	(0.3)
Chinese Taipei	78.1	(1.2)	91.5	(2.1)	54.0	(1.6)	74.4	(3.7)	80.4	(0.9)	94.1	(1.9)	67.0	(1.2)	83.4	(2.8)
Turkey	40.8	(1.3)	48.5	(0.9)	25.9	(1.1)	41.8	(0.8)	54.6	(1.5)	74.2	(0.8)	50.0	(1.4)	67.7	(0.8)

(continued)

6.2 Curriculum and Pedagogy

Table 6.3 (continued)

	Percentage of teachers working in a school with diverse ethnic and cultural student background[1] where the following diversity-related practices are implemented															
	Supporting activities or organizations encouraging students' expression of diverse ethnic and cultural identities				Organizing multicultural events				Teaching how to deal with ethnic and cultural discrimination				Adopting teaching and learning practices that integrate global issues throughout the curriculum			
	According to teachers		According to principals[2]		According to teachers		According to principals[2]		According to teachers		According to principals[2]		According to teachers		According to principals[2]	
	%	S.E.	%	S.E.	%	S.E.	%	S.E.	%	S.E.	%	S.E.	%	S.E.	%	S.E.
United Arab Emirates	88.1	(0.6)	94.4	(0.2)	89.8	(0.5)	96.1	(0.3)	84.0	(0.6)	94.8	(0.2)	88.3	(0.6)	94.6	(0.2)
United States	72.8	(2.5)	90.2	(2.7)	52.1	(3.9)	73.1	(5.3)	62.8	(2.4)	79.9	(4.1)	66.9	(2.5)	83.6	(4.0)
Vietnam	94.8	(1.2)	93.5	(3.0)	71.3	(2.6)	70.0	(6.5)	91.7	(1.1)	88.5	(4.1)	91.6	(1.2)	88.5	(4.6)
OECD average-30	54.2	(0.4)	61.3	(0.8)	45.4	(0.5)	55.3	(0.8)	70.1	(0.3)	79.8	(0.7)	68.0	(0.3)	79.9	(0.7)
EU total-23	57.0	(0.5)	67.0	(1.2)	41.9	(0.6)	54.5	(1.3)	74.6	(0.4)	82.7	(0.9)	72.7	(0.4)	84.4	(0.9)
TALIS average-47	62.7	(0.3)	69.9	(0.6)	54.2	(0.4)	64.0	(0.7)	73.1	(0.2)	82.5	(0.6)	70.2	(0.2)	80.2	(0.6)
Australia[a]	81.4	(1.0)	85.1	(0.1)	75.1	(1.0)	88.6	(0.2)	68.6	(1.0)	76.1	(0.2)	82.7	(0.9)	88.1	(0.2)

Source OECD (2019a, Table I.3.35)

Table 6.4 Teaching in multicultural or multilingual settings

- Countries/economies where the indicator is **above** the OECD average
- Countries/economies where the indicator is **not statistically different** from the OECD average
- Countries/economies where the indicator is **below** the OECD average

	Percentage of teachers teaching in classes with more than 10% of students whose first language is different from the language of instruction	Percentage of teachers for whom "teaching in a multicultural or multilingual setting" was included in their formal education or training	Percentage of teachers who felt "well prepared" or "very well prepared" for teaching in a multicultural or multilingual setting	Percentage of teachers for whom "teaching in a multicultural or multilingual setting" was included in their recent professional development activities	Percentage of teachers reporting a high level of need for professional development in teaching in a multicultural or multilingual setting	Percentage of teachers who feel they can cope with the challenges of a multicultural classroom "quite a bit" or "a lot" in teaching a culturally diverse class[a]
Alberta (Canada)	45	63	38	41	10	67
Australia	27	59	27	23	7	70
Austria	42	31	15	18	14	74
Belgium	35	31	16	13	9	81
– Flemish Comm. (*Belgium*)	39	34	17	18	8	77
Brazil	4	42	44	27	44	81
Bulgaria	40	27	26	31	21	82
CABA (Argentina)	9	35	34	19	25	70
Chile	5	42	37	21	34	57
Colombia	5	47	30	29	45	90
Croatia	8	25	20	19	14	81
Czech Republic	3	16	10	14	6	65
Denmark	21	37	26	14	11	85
England (UK)	27	68	43	19	5	72
Estonia	13	28	16	25	11	70
Finland	15	29	14	20	7	69
France	16	12	8	6	17	66
Georgia	9	30	33	35	12	71
Hungary	2	19	28	15	13	84
Iceland	24	27	13	23	19	62
Israel*	17	34	33	21	17	63
Italy	17	26	19	28	14	80
Japan	2	27	11	13	15	17
Kazakhstan	33	48	43	37	13	68
Korea	4	29	24	31	14	31
Latvia	23	33	32	28	11	89
Lithuania	6	23	35	18	10	67
Malta	29	38	23	27	20	65

(continued)

6.2 Curriculum and Pedagogy

Table 6.4 (continued)

	Percentage of teachers teaching in classes with more than 10% of students whose first language is different from the language of instruction	Percentage of teachers for whom "teaching in a multicultural or multilingual setting" was included in their formal education or training	Percentage of teachers who felt "well prepared" or "very well prepared" for teaching in a multicultural or multilingual setting	Percentage of teachers for whom "teaching in a multicultural or multilingual setting" was included in their recent professional development activities	Percentage of teachers reporting a high level of need for professional development in teaching in a multicultural or multilingual setting	Percentage of teachers who feel they can cope with the challenges of a multicultural classroom "quite a bit" or "a lot" in teaching a culturally diverse class[a]
Mexico	4	27	26	16	46	59
Netherlands	15	30	17	10	4	68
New Zealand	27	78	45	46	7	74
Norway	23	29	15	15	13	59
Portugal	8	21	19	14	22	94
Romania	8	37	43	22	27	72
Russian Federation	12	31	32	24	13	83
Saudi Arabia	11	36	43	40	26	77
Shanghai (China)	3	63	52	43	22	45
Singapore	58	72	61	25	5	65
Slovak Republic	11	26	21	14	9	64
Slovenia	16	12	27	18	14	58
South Africa	62	75	67	54	20	81
Spain	22	29	26	32	18	52
Sweden	41	41	32	24	15	68
Turkey	18	33	39	27	22	55
United Arab Emirates	50	76	80	65	10	90
United States	25	70	48	42	6	66
Viet Nam	20	44	31	41	19	46
OECD average-31	18	35	26	22	15	67

[a]The sample is restricted to teachers reporting that they have already taught a classroom with students from different cultures

Source OECD, TALIS 2018 Database, Tables I.3.28, I.4.13, I.4.20, I.5.18, I.5.21, and I.3.38
Information on data for Israel: https://oe.cd/israel-disclaimer. OECD (2019a, Fig. I.1.2)

Table 6.5 Teachers' needs for professional development. *Results based on responses of lower secondary teachers*

	Teaching in a multicultural or multilingual setting		Teaching cross-curricular skills[3]		Communicating with people from different cultures or countries	
	%	S.E.	%	S.E.	%	S.E.
Alberta (Canada)	9.6	(1.8)	5.8	(0.8)	4.4	(0.7)
Australia	7.2	(0.5)	8.9	(0.7)	3.7	(0.5)
Austria	13.8	(0.7)	11.3	(0.6)	9.4	(0.6)
Belgium	9.3	(0.5)	7.1	(0.5)	5.5	(0.4)
– Flemish Comm. (*Belgium*)	8.4	(0.8)	5.1	(0.5)	3.8	(0.5)
Brazil	44.0	(1.3)	17.4	(0.9)	40.9	(1.3)
Bulgaria	21.2	(1.0)	12.2	(0.8)	18.5	(0.9)
CABA (Argentina)	24.9	(1.3)	8.9	(0.8)	14.8	(0.8)
Chile	33.8	(1.2)	21.2	(1.0)	26.4	(1.0)
Colombia	45.4	(1.5)	26.3	(1.4)	40.1	(1.3)
Croatia	14.3	(1.0)	23.4	(0.8)	15.1	(0.8)
Cyprus	19.6	(1.2)	11.9	(1.1)	13.5	(0.9)
Czech Republic	6.5	(0.5)	9.3	(0.6)	6.1	(0.4)
Denmark	10.7	(0.9)	9.0	(0.7)	5.2	(0.6)
England (UK)	4.9	(0.5)	3.4	(0.4)	2.9	(0.4)
Estonia	10.5	(0.8)	17.2	(0.7)	8.4	(0.6)
Finland	6.9	(0.6)	6.0	(0.5)	4.4	(0.5)
France	16.7	(0.8)	13.6	(0.7)	12.0	(0.8)
Georgia	12.4	(0.8)	20.1	(0.9)	17.3	(0.9)
Hungary	12.6	(0.7)	13.6	(0.8)	9.8	(0.6)
Iceland	19.4	(1.1)	10.1	(0.8)	9.5	(0.9)
Israel	16.5	(1.0)	25.3	(1.1)	15.2	(0.9)
Italy	14.4	(0.6)	12.9	(0.7)	11.9	(0.7)
Japan	14.9	(0.8)	31.8	(0.9)	15.9	(0.8)
Kazakhstan	12.7	(0.5)	18.4	(0.7)	11.8	(0.6)
Korea	14.5	(0.9)	26.2	(1.0)	13.8	(0.8)
Latvia	11.1	(1.1)	17.4	(1.2)	10.6	(0.8)
Lithuania	9.5	(0.5)	18.7	(0.8)	10.1	(0.5)
Malta	20.4	(1.2)	15.2	(0.8)	12.2	(0.7)
Mexico	45.9	(1.3)	13.6	(0.8)	31.9	(1.0)
Netherlands	3.6	(0.5)	12.4	(1.1)	2.6	(0.4)
New Zealand	7.3	(0.8)	11.7	(0.8)	4.0	(0.6)

(continued)

6.2 Curriculum and Pedagogy

Table 6.5 (continued)

	Teaching in a multicultural or multilingual setting		Teaching cross-curricular skills[3]		Communicating with people from different cultures or countries	
	%	S.E.	%	S.E.	%	S.E.
Norway	12.6	(0.8)	12.8	(0.6)	6.4	(0.5)
Portugal	21.6	(0.8)	11.3	(0.6)	11.5	(0.6)
Romania	27.1	(1.0)	22.8	(0.8)	27.4	(1.0)
Russia	12.7	(0.8)	15.1	(0.8)	13.7	(0.9)
Saudi Arabia	26.0	(1.2)	25.7	(1.2)	30.3	(1.3)
Shanghai (China)	22.0	(0.9)	30.0	(1.0)	19.2	(0.7)
Singapore	5.4	(0.4)	15.2	(0.7)	4.1	(0.4)
Slovak Republic	9.3	(0.6)	16.3	(0.7)	8.2	(0.6)
Slovenia	14.3	(1.0)	10.6	(0.7)	7.8	(0.6)
South Africa	19.9	(1.2)	15.2	(1.1)	21.2	(1.3)
Spain	17.6	(0.6)	15.6	(0.6)	11.2	(0.5)
Sweden	14.8	(0.7)	8.0	(0.7)	7.1	(0.6)
Chinese Taipei	12.4	(0.7)	26.1	(0.8)	9.9	(0.6)
Turkey	22.2	(0.8)	7.4	(0.6)	24.6	(0.9)
United Arab Emirates	10.1	(0.4)	9.5	(0.3)	9.8	(0.3)
United States	6.1	(1.1)	6.2	(0.6)	4.7	(0.9)
Vietnam	19.1	(1.5)	66.2	(1.2)	19.0	(1.1)
OECD average-31	15.0	(0.2)	13.6	(0.1)	11.1	(0.1)
EU total-23	13.4	(0.2)	12.1	(0.2)	9.9	(0.2)
TALIS average-48	16.4	(0.1)	16.1	(0.1)	13.4	(0.1)

Source OECD (2019a, Table I.5.21)

The OECD study of teachers documents that on average, across the countries participating, 13% of the principals report incidents of bullying in their schools, as shown in Table 6.6. In the United States, the Southern Poverty Law Center has documented the prevalence of discrimination and hatred in schools. In a survey administered in 2018, more than two-thirds of the teachers and principals surveyed had witnessed a hate or bias incident the previous semester, but less than 5% of those were reported by news media. Most of these incidents were not addressed by school leaders: in 57% of the cases no one was disciplined, and only 10% of the administrators denounced the bias or reaffirmed school values in response to it (Southern Poverty Law Center 2019).

Innovative curriculum and pedagogies for global education should not simply be an "add on" to the existing curriculum, but an avenue to transform the curriculum and pedagogy broadly, in service on supporting deeper learning and twenty-first-century skills. Clearly, these competencies and the associated pedagogies of

Table 6.6 School safety. *Results based on responses of lower secondary principals*

	Intimidation or bullying among students[a]		Physical injury caused by violence among students		A student or parent/guardian reports postings of hurtful information on the Internet about students	
	%	S.E.	%	S.E.	%	S.E.
Alberta (Canada)	12.5	(3.4)	0.7	(0.7)	3.9	(1.8)
Austria	15.0	(3.0)	0.7	(0.4)	3.2	(1.3)
Belgium	35.6	(3.4)	1.2	(0.7)	9.2	(1.7)
– Flemish Comm. (Belgium)	40.3	(4.3)	0.4	(0.4)	9.2	(2.3)
Brazil	28.3	(3.6)	8.8	(2.4)	2.4	(1.2)
Bulgaria	25.6	(3.6)	5.4	(1.9)	0.2	(0.2)
CABA (Argentina)	4.6	(1.5)	0.8	(0.8)	3.1	(1.8)
Chile	3.7	(1.5)	1.9	(1.1)	0.0	(0.0)
Colombia	15.2	(3.6)	4.3	(2.3)	1.8	(1.4)
Croatia	3.8	(1.2)	0.0	(0.0)	0.8	(0.6)
Cyprus	16.2	(3.2)	5.1	(2.3)	1.0	(1.0)
Czech Republic	2.9	(1.2)	0.0	(0.0)	0.2	(0.2)
Denmark	4.6	(1.8)	0.9	(0.6)	0.0	(0.0)
England (UK)	20.7	(3.4)	2.6	(1.2)	13.9	(2.8)
Estonia	12.0	(2.3)	0.0	(0.0)	1.6	(0.9)
Finland	29.4	(4.0)	2.3	(1.2)	0.0	(0.0)
France	26.8	(3.4)	2.4	(1.1)	4.2	(1.4)
Georgia	1.5	(0.9)	0.0	(0.0)	0.3	(0.3)
Hungary	10.2	(2.7)	2.0	(1.0)	1.9	(1.2)
Iceland	2.2	(1.5)	0.0	(0.0)	1.1	(1.1)
Israel	26.2	(3.4)	13.1	(2.5)	1.6	(1.1)
Italy	3.2	(1.1)	0.2	(0.2)	0.8	(0.5)
Japan	0.4	(0.4)	0.4	(0.4)	0.5	(0.4)
Kazakhstan	0.6	(0.4)	0.0	(0.0)	0.0	(0.0)
Korea	0.4	(0.4)	0.4	(0.4)	0.0	(0.0)
Latvia	9.0	(3.1)	0.4	(0.4)	0.3	(0.3)
Lithuania	18.2	(3.0)	0.0	(0.0)	0.0	(0.0)
Malta	30.0	(7.3)	7.7	(3.9)	6.2	(3.6)
Mexico	16.9	(2.6)	5.9	(1.4)	2.5	(1.0)
Netherlands	12.9	(2.8)	0.0	(0.0)	5.2	(2.1)
New Zealand	34.6	(8.7)	4.2	(1.9)	4.3	(1.1)
Norway	14.8	(3.2)	0.0	(0.0)	0.9	(0.6)
Portugal	7.3	(1.9)	3.1	(1.2)	0.0	(0.0)

(continued)

Table 6.6 (continued)

	Intimidation or bullying among students[a]		Physical injury caused by violence among students		A student or parent/guardian reports postings of hurtful information on the Internet about students	
	%	S.E.	%	S.E.	%	S.E.
Romania	13.5	(3.3)	1.8	(0.9)	1.5	(1.2)
Russia	2.0	(1.7)	0.0	(0.0)	0.0	(0.0)
Saudi Arabia	10.1	(2.7)	3.5	(1.8)	0.4	(0.4)
Shanghai (China)	0.0	(0.0)	0.0	(0.0)	0.0	(0.0)
Singapore	4.3	(1.5)	0.0	(0.0)	3.3	(1.5)
Slovak Republic	9.0	(2.2)	0.6	(0.6)	0.0	(0.0)
Slovenia	13.7	(3.1)	1.1	(1.1)	0.7	(0.7)
South Africa	34.4	(4.3)	6.2	(1.6)	1.9	(1.0)
Spain	5.0	(1.2)	0.5	(0.3)	1.2	(0.7)
Sweden	26.0	(9.2)	1.7	(1.0)	4.6	(2.0)
Chinese Taipei	0.3	(0.3)	0.0	(0.0)	0.0	(0.0)
Turkey	13.3	(2.6)	7.5	(2.8)	0.2	(0.2)
United Arab Emirates	8.0	(1.3)	1.1	(0.5)	0.7	(0.4)
United States	27.3	(9.9)	0.8	(0.4)	10.2	(2.9)
Vietnam	1.8	(1.0)	0.0	(0.0)	0.0	(0.0)
OECD average-30	14.3	(0.7)	2.0	(0.2)	2.5	(0.2)
EU total-23	13.8	(0.8)	1.4	(0.2)	2.9	(0.4)
TALIS average-47	13.1	(0.5)	2.1	(0.2)	2.0	(0.2)
Australia[c]	37.2	(6.2)	7.2	(2.5)	10.6	(2.5)

[a]Or other forms of verbal abuse
[b]For example, via texts, e-mails or online
Source OECD (2019a, Table I.3.42)

student-centered, active, collaborative, and project-based learning could be used in a range of subjects, and do not need an explicit emphasis on global education to be promoted or supported. Introducing these practices in the context of a global education curriculum, however, provides a framing of this process of pedagogical change that does not require confronting head on the established norms and mindsets with respect to teaching the existing disciplines in the curriculum, but rather can begin the conversation laterally, using a new framing to discuss teaching and learning in service of helping students develop the skills to achieve the Sustainable Development Goals. Data from the OECD study of teachers suggest that most teachers are open to educational innovation, as shown in Table 6.7. On average, among all countries

Table 6.7 Teachers' views on their colleagues' attitudes towards innovation. *Results based on responses of lower secondary teachers*

	Percentage of teachers who "agree" or "strongly agree" with the following statements			
	Most teachers in the school strive to develop new ideas for teaching and learning (%)	Most teachers in the school are open to change (%)	Most teachers in the school search for new ways to solve problems (%)	Most teachers in the school provide practical support to each other for the application of new ideas (%)
Alberta (Canada)	86.1	79.0	81.9	85.9
Australia	83.2	74.4	74.8	84.2
Austria	82.0	71.1	71.2	77.4
Belgium	68.1	61.1	65.9	64.7
– Flemish Comm. (Belgium)	69.8	63.7	71.4	76.5
Brazil	84.4	80.0	83.7	80.0
Bulgaria	86.2	88.0	83.7	86.3
CABA (Argentina)	83.3	75.4	82.5	80.0
Chile	79.7	71.9	75.1	72.0
Colombia	83.3	76.1	80.9	77.7
Croatia	73.7	70.8	71.4	72.4
Cyprus	64.0	65.6	69.9	73.0
Czech Republic	67.6	68.3	71.7	76.7
Denmark	82.0	77.6	77.3	86.5
England (UK)	82.1	76.0	76.6	84.2
Estonia	74.0	82.1	79.3	78.1
Finland	79.1	68.7	74.4	74.9
France	76.7	69.1	67.7	73.5
Georgia	91.6	91.9	92.0	93.2
Hungary	86.0	80.4	82.5	81.0
Iceland	81.1	78.2	82.4	82.9
Israel	72.7	69.9	73.0	78.4
Italy	73.4	69.9	72.6	74.4
Japan	81.7	70.1	77.5	70.6
Kazakhstan	90.4	84.7	90.1	92.6
Korea	86.6	69.8	79.4	70.9

(continued)

6.2 Curriculum and Pedagogy

Table 6.7 (continued)

	Percentage of teachers who "agree" or "strongly agree" with the following statements			
	Most teachers in the school strive to develop new ideas for teaching and learning (%)	Most teachers in the school are open to change (%)	Most teachers in the school search for new ways to solve problems (%)	Most teachers in the school provide practical support to each other for the application of new ideas (%)
Latvia	89.4	86.1	86.8	85.3
Lithuania	88.8	86.1	87.7	83.8
Malta	78.2	67.1	77.8	79.8
Mexico	82.3	76.0	80.9	70.9
Netherlands	64.0	67.4	64.6	71.4
New Zealand	79.8	73.1	75.0	82.7
Norway	72.1	80.7	92.6	84.9
Portugal	64.8	59.3	66.4	65.5
Romania	86.9	85.5	85.7	83.2
Russia	77.8	84.7	84.0	86.1
Saudi Arabia	85.1	85.0	85.6	84.4
Shanghai (China)	91.7	89.2	90.6	91.6
Singapore	78.9	74.5	73.8	84.1
Slovak Republic	82.2	80.7	78.8	83.3
Slovenia	85.2	79.8	80.6	81.2
South Africa	70.1	78.7	78.7	76.2
Spain	75.9	68.7	73.0	71.4
Sweden	74.5	74.9	75.8	78.5
Chinese Taipei	74.7	73.5	80.7	77.3
Turkey	80.7	79.2	80.3	79.4
United Arab Emirates	89.2	87.2	88.5	88.7
United States	83.5	70.5	75.4	83.8
Vietnam	94.2	89.5	93.9	93.9
OECD average-31	79.0	74.1	76.8	77.9
EU total-23	77.0	72.2	73.6	76.4
TALIS average-48	80.2	76.4	79.1	80.0

Source OECD (2019a, Table I.2.35)

participating in the study, four in five teachers are looking for new ideas for teaching and learning, three-quarters of teachers report that they are open to change, and four in five teachers are in search of new ways to solve problems.

6.3 Instructional Resources

As with other subjects, effective teaching can be supported by high-quality resources, textbooks, and online resources that engage students in structured opportunities to develop skills. Critical resources include the school infrastructure—the building itself—and technology infrastructure. These resources support learning in many ways. For example, schools can be "green spaces" and minimize their carbon footprint, which is not only a way to mitigate climate change but teaches students important lessons on how to live to minimize our impact on climate. In 2008, Australia adopted a national solar schools initiative with a major component to mitigate climate change. The initiative makes grants available to schools to put in place energy and water efficiency measures (UNESCO 2012, p. 13). Japan also has had a program of environmentally friendly schools since 1997 (Ibid, p. 16).

Access to technology, for teachers and for students, is another important resource which can support student work and the creation of collaborations with peers in other schools. There are a number of sites online which allow students to collaborate with peers, such as worldvuze, touchable earth, flat connections, global read aloud, or write the world (Klein 2017). The Global Citizen platform has many online resources to support learning and projects aligned with the UN Sustainable Development Goals. The UN also has resources online for the same purpose, as does the World's Largest Lesson.

One of the findings of a cross-national study of reforms that broadened the curriculum in ten different countries is that many had relied on the use of tools, protocols, and textbooks to support the adoption of new instructional practices (Reimers 2020a). The same was found in a cross-national study of six national programs of teacher professional development, they relied on instructional materials to provide day-to-day support to new pedagogies (Reimers 2020b). This was also what we found in a comparative study of professional development programs aimed at educating the whole child (Reimers 2018).

There are numerous resources available online that can support global education, including textbooks or resource books addressing globalization and global themes, such as the recently published book 'The World. A Brief Introduction' (Haass 2020). Part of the process of advancing global education requires examining whether textbook use supports it. An analysis of secondary history, social science and geography textbooks between 1970 and 2008 found that mentions of international events increased from 30 to 40%, and globalization, almost not mentioned in 1970, was mentioned in 40% of the textbooks in 2005. Analysis conducted by UNESCO of textbooks in history, civics, social studies, and geography showed that about 50% mention human rights, compared to about 5% at the beginning of the twentieth century. About 28% of the textbooks mention international human rights documents.

6.3 Instructional Resources

Coverage of women's rights is much more uneven, from just about 10% in Northern Africa and Western Asia to 40% in Europe, North America and Sub-Saharan Africa. About 50% of the textbooks mention environmental issues (UNESCO 2017, p. 295).

Because finding what is needed when it is needed is time-consuming, organized collections can be especially helpful. Curating these and aligning them to standards and curriculum is a way to support global education. Various states and countries have developed websites which host curated lists of resources keyed to standards or to curriculum. Education Services Australia has created such a site, with resources aligned to the curriculum and to various pedagogical strategies (Education Services Australia 2019).

The organization High Resolves has also curated a range of education resources, with an application that allows teachers to re-purpose and re-organize those resources to align them to particular curricular goals (High Resolves 2019).

The organization Facing History and Ourselves has curated a collection of teaching strategies and instructional resources to support the promotion of tolerance, empathy, personal responsibility, and teaching history including Holocaust education (Facing History and Ourselves 2019).

UNESCO has also curated a variety of resources to support global education and teaching for sustainability (UNESCO 2019a, b).

When we developed the World Course, we deliberately chose not to develop specific lesson plans, but instead develop a curriculum at the level of "units." The 350 units of the K-12 curriculum could then be developed into several lessons each. While we suggested activities and resources for each unit, we refrained from structuring specific lessons. We were able to identify thousands of resources on the internet that could support the development of lessons within each of the units. Our assumption was that teachers would benefit from and appreciate the flexibility of designing their own lesson plans to fit the particular circumstances and needs of their students. The feedback I have received from those using the book indicates that designing lesson plans takes time and skill, and that competing demands for teachers often prevent them from doing this. For this reason, the subsequent curriculum I developed with my graduate students "Empowering Students to Improve the World in Sixty Lessons" included sixty lesson plans. The feedback from teachers to having structured lessons, which they can then modify and adapt, has been very positive.

6.4 Assessment

Assessment is an important component in an institutional perspective because it provides evidence on how the intended curriculum translates into a taught or implemented curriculum and eventuallly into a learned or achieved curriculum. Where that evidence is used to hold teachers and schools accountable, it has powerful effects on instruction, as demonstrated by a study of the effects of test-based accountability in the United States which showed that the introduction of accountability emphasizing basic literacies, resulted in an increase in instructional time in literacy and mathematics and in a decrease in instructional time in science and social studies (West 2007, 54). A common misconception is that one of the obstacles to advancing global education is that it is not a domain typically assessed or where assessment is feasible. One of the findings of the comparative study of effective programs to develop the capacity of teachers to educate the whole child conducted by the Global Education Innovation Initiative (Reimers and Chung 2018) is that these programs typically focus on a broader range of skills than those normally assessed in state or national assessments. However, one of the features these programs had in common was a commitment to monitoring and evaluation as a way to continuously improve, which often required using additional assessment tools than those used for accountability purposes.

Because global competence is a construct encompassing a combination of knowledge and skills, a productive way to identify relevant assessments is to focus on those components of global competency, not necessarily to look for global education assessments. For example, foreign language proficiency is one of those components, and there are established metrics to assess foreign language skills. Similarly, a number of the components of global competency fall squarely within existing disciplines such as world history, social studies, geography, and science, and there are well-developed modes of formative and summative assessments in those disciplines.

For instance, knowledge and understanding of climate and the underlying science can be reliably assessed. The Program for International Student Assessment, administered by the OECD, shows that, on average, only one in five students in the OECD countries can consistently identify, explain and apply scientific concepts related to environmental topics (OECD 2012). Conversely, 16% of the students do not have enough knowledge to answer questions containing scientific information related to basic environmental issues, and 20% of the students are just at that baseline level of scientific proficiency. These low levels of scientific knowledge and skills are in spite of the fact that all students in the OECD attend schools teaching environmental science as part of the science curriculum. The latest administration of the PISA study revealed that less than 10% of all students tested could distinguish facts from opinions (OECD 2019b, p. 3).

There is a rich reservoir of assessment instruments which can be used to evaluate other dimensions of global citizenship education such as intercultural competency or global mindedness. The Intercultural Development Inventory assesses the capability to shift cultural perspective and adapt to cultural differences and commonalities. Another instrument, the Intercultural Effectiveness Scale, assesses the skills critical to interacting effectively across cultures. The General Ethnocentrism Survey measures how individuals construe "in-group" versus "outgroups." The Global Citizenship Literacy Scale measures global awareness, intergroup empathy, valuing diversity, social justice, environmental sustainability and responsibility to act.

In addition, assessment instruments used to measure civic skills and values can provide information on competencies that constitute part of global citizenship. The World Values Survey Project, which has administered cross-national surveys on cultural values for decades, contains accepted metrics of constructs such as tolerance for diversity, attitudes towards the environment and various civic and political topics. Similarly, the International Association for the Evaluation of Educational Achievement has, since the 1960s, conducted cross-national assessments of civic knowledge and skills. More recently, the inclusion of an assessment of global competency by the PISA program of the OECD will bring additional focus to the aspects of this competency reflected in that assessment.

Assessment can also focus on teacher knowledge, attitudes, and practices. For instance, Kerkhoff developed a scale to assess teaching for global readiness, which identifies four elements of pedagogy drawn from a factor analysis of teachers' self-reports of their practices, based on a review of the literature on global education (Kerkhoff 2017).

A working group co-convened by UNESCO, The Center for Universal Education at the Brookings Institution and the UN Global Education First Initiative Youth Advocacy Group assembled a toolkit with fifty assessment instruments (Center for Universal Education 2017). These instruments focus on three distinct domains "(1) fostering the values/attitudes of being an agent of positive change; (2) building knowledge of where, why, and how to take action toward positive change; and (3) developing self-efficacy for taking effective actions toward positive change" (Ibid, p. 11).

6.5 Staff and Development

One of the reasons global education is too often an aspiration for teachers and seldom a reality for students is because more time has been spent examining what it is than discerning how to teach it. As mentioned earlier in this book, much of the existent literature on the subject are academic discussions about competing views of what global competency means. If the studies on how to teach for global competency are few, research on how teachers can be supported to effectively educate globally competent students is woefully lacking. Clearly, effective global education pedagogy will not be possible if teachers and principals are not prepared to lead good instruction.

What is necessary is obvious: explicit high-quality initial preparation for teachers, and good professional development throughout teachers' careers. These are the same requirements consistently mentioned in any study and proposal to advance twenty-first-century education and deeper learning (Aspen Institute 2019; Pellegrino and Hilton 2012; Reimers et al. 2016; Reimers and Chung 2018).

> Current systems of teacher preparation and professional development will require major changes if they are to support teaching that encourages deeper learning and the development of transferable competencies. Changes will need to be made not only in conception of what constitutes effective professional practice but also in the purposes, structure, and organization of preservice and professional learning opportunities. (Pellegrino and Hilton 2012, p. 186)

Following Schon's ideas summarized earlier, effective teacher education and professional development need to incorporate opportunities for practice, and opportunities to learn from practice. The knowledge base to educate globally competent students needs to be built, in part, by teachers themselves. Thus, teacher education programs must engage students in practice, and in reflection on and research from practice, to prepare them to participate in systems of continuous improvement, as proposed by Bryk and his colleagues (Bryk et al. 2015). A tighter coupling between initial education and professional support once teachers are in school would also support this two-way continuum from education to practice.

Initial teacher education should also provide teachers with the knowledge and the skills that encompass global education, including skills to teach foreign languages, develop the intercultural sensibilities of their students, promote civic engagement, teach about climate, sustainability, world history, geography, globalization, and other globally relevant themes. One challenge faced by teacher education programs in addressing these areas is that to do so effectively would require augmenting the capacity of faculty in teacher education programs. For university-based programs this could be done by developing more robust collaborations with other academic departments, for example with sciences, history, modern languages, or economics. Unfortunately, many teacher preparation programs occupy a relatively marginal place in schools of education, and in turn schools of education rarely develop curriculum or professional development in collaboration with colleagues from other university departments or professional schools.

A recent analysis of the role of education for sustainable development in the curriculum of teacher education institutions conducted in 66 countries found that barely 8% of the programs had integrated sustainable development in the curriculum (McKeown and Hopkins 2014). A survey of student teachers in a teacher preparation program in Wales, Bangor, found that while most student teachers recognize the importance of global education, few of them felt prepared to introduce this in their teaching. Among those surveyed, 59% thought global citizenship should have a higher priority in the primary school curriculum, 76% thought it should have a higher priority in the secondary school curriculum, and 64% thought it should have a high priority in initial teacher training. However, only 35% felt confidence in a whole-school approach to global citizenship and 31% felt confident to contribute to a whole-school approach to sustainable development (Robbin et al. 2003, p. 96). A study of global education in teacher training colleges in a province in the Netherlands showed that the meaning of global citizenship was vague for faculty and there was great variation in identifying a number of related subthemes as part of global citizenship (Van Werven 2012). A study of the integration of global content and co-curricular cross-cultural experiences in teacher preparation programs at a large public university in Florida found that a small percentage of teacher candidates participated in those courses and experiences, even though participation increased global perspectives. Two-thirds of students had taken no foreign language courses, two in five had taken one or no courses focusing on other countries and regions, 69% had taken no international or comparative courses and 25% had taken no classes that provided opportunities for intercultural dialogue (Poole 2014, pp. 49–50). A study of the role of human rights education in Denmark found that it was poorly implemented in schools and in teacher education programs:

This study shows that it is arbitrary whether pupils in primary and lower secondary schools in Denmark learn about rights of the child. It also shows that human rights are not incorporated adequately in the official curriculum at schools and teacher university colleges. An overall finding of the study is that teachers have insufficient frameworks and tools for creating quality in education when it comes to human rights education…87% the teachers respond that their teacher education did not motivate them at all, or motivated them only to a lesser extent, to teach pupils about human rights. (Danish Institute for Human Rights 2014, pp. 1–2)

Teacher education programs should also help teacher candidates develop their own intercultural and global competency, for instance, structuring cohorts which are culturally diverse, engaging students in exchanges with peers in other countries, using technology or via study abroad. Research on semester-long teaching abroad, however, shows that it does not guarantee the development of global knowledge or of intercultural skills (Ibid, p. 203). A study of the impact of a semester of teaching abroad for American student teachers shows that their intercultural competence increased. At the same time, they did not learn to see teaching as culturally based (Ibid, p. 209, 210). Student teachers from Hong Kong who participated in a six-week program of student teaching in New Zealand reported that this experience had enriched their cultural understanding, pedagogical knowledge and skills, language awareness, and classroom awareness (Lee 2011). Similar findings are reported in a study of 40 student teachers from a university in the Midwest of the United States who student taught abroad and reported enhanced global awareness and ability to consider themes from multiple perspectives. Teaching overseas also increased their employability and their ability to include cross-cultural content in their curriculum (Doppen and An 2014, p. 72).

These benefits of study abroad for teachers and teacher candidates contrast with the lack of study or travel abroad experiences of teachers around the world, as documented in an OECD study of teachers, as shown in Table 6.8. The result of such lack of travel is that teachers lack cross-cultural knowledge and experience. In the United States "teacher education students tend to be cross-culturally inexperienced and globally unaware, making it difficult for them to effectively address the differentiated needs in today's classrooms" (Boynton-Haueerwas et al. 2017, p. 202).

A study examining the participation of teacher candidates in online project-based collaborations reported various benefits in student engagement, development of professional relationships and motivation to pursue further global projects (Smith 2014).

A report on teacher preparation for global education produced by an expert group convened by the Longview Foundation provides the following framework to improve initial teacher education:

Framework for Internationalizing Teacher Preparation

1. Revising teacher preparation programs to ensure that:
    a. General education coursework helps each prospective teacher develop a deep knowledge of at least one world region, culture, or global issue, and facility in one language in addition to English.
    b. Professional education courses teach the pedagogical skills to enable future teachers to teach the global dimensions of their subject matter.

Table 6.8 Teacher study abroad during teacher education. *Results based on responses of lower secondary teachers*

	Percentage of teachers who studied abroad as a student, as part of their teacher education		Percentage of teachers who have been abroad only as a student, as part of their teacher education (a)	
	%	S.E.	%	S.E.
Alberta (Canada)	10.1	(1.3)	5.2	(0.8)
Australia	A	a	a	a
Austria	A	a	a	a
Belgium	26.9	(0.7)	14.7	(0.6)
– *Flemish Comm. (Belgium)*	27.1	(0.8)	15.1	(0.8)
Brazil	A	a	a	a
Bulgaria	12.7	(0.8)	6.4	(0.5)
CABA (Argentina)	A	a	a	a
Chile	8.2	(0.8)	2.9	(0.4)
Colombia	7.5	(0.9)	3.6	(0.4)
Croatia	16.7	(0.7)	6.7	(0.4)
Cyprus	44.7	(1.4)	16.0	(1.0)
Czech Republic	21.5	(0.8)	7.3	(0.5)
Denmark	34.7	(1.2)	13.5	(0.9)
England (UK)	10.2	(0.6)	3.6	(0.5)
Estonia	14.8	(0.8)	3.3	(0.4)
Finland	21.4	(0.8)	6.7	(0.6)
France	16.8	(0.8)	5.2	(0.5)
Georgia	5.9	(0.5)	2.2	(0.3)
Hungary	18.0	(0.8)	7.8	(0.6)
Iceland	21.5	(1.3)	2.5	(0.4)
Israel	A	a	a	a
Italy	28.6	(0.7)	14.0	(0.6)
Japan	A	a	a	a
Kazakhstan	5.8	(0.3)	2.7	(0.2)
Korea	A	a	a	a
Latvia	9.9	(1.2)	1.9	(0.7)
Lithuania	A	a	a	a
Malta	13.6	(0.9)	5.4	(0.6)
Mexico	6.6	(0.6)	2.9	(0.4)
Netherlands	36.6	(1.4)	12.0	(0.8)

(continued)

Table 6.8 (continued)

	Percentage of teachers who studied abroad as a student, as part of their teacher education		Percentage of teachers who have been abroad only as a student, as part of their teacher education (a)	
	%	S.E.	%	S.E.
New Zealand	A	a	a	a
Norway	A	a	a	a
Portugal	8.9	(0.5)	2.7	(0.3)
Romania	8.9	(0.8)	3.3	(0.3)
Russia	2.6	(0.3)	1.1	(0.2)
Saudi Arabia	6.6	(0.6)	1.2	(0.3)
Shanghai (China)	6.1	(0.4)	1.9	(0.2)
Singapore	A	a	a	a
Slovak Republic	16.7	(0.7)	7.9	(0.5)
Slovenia	16.1	(0.9)	4.0	(0.5)
South Africa	9.9	(1.1)	0.5	(0.2)
Spain	28.8	(0.7)	9.1	(0.5)
Sweden	22.5	(1.0)	9.8	(0.7)
Chinese Taipei	12.4	(0.7)	3.0	(0.3)
Turkey	2.8	(0.3)	0.9	(0.2)
United Arab Emirates	17.2	(0.5)	3.6	(0.3)
United States	A	a	a	a
Vietnam	1.0	(0.2)	0.1	(0.0)

Source OECD (2019a, Table I.4.23)

  c. Field experiences support the development of pre-service teachers' global perspectives.
2. Facilitating at least one in-depth cross-cultural experience for every pre-service teacher by:
  a. Promoting study or student teaching in another country, or service-learning or student teaching in a multicultural community in the United States.
  b. Financial support for such experiences.
  c. Appropriate orientation, supervision, and debriefing to tie these experiences to prospective teachers' emerging teaching practice.
3. Modernizing and expanding programs for prospective world language teachers by:
  a. Preparing more teachers to teach less commonly taught languages.
  b. Updating language education pedagogy based on current research and best practice.
4. Creating formative and summative assessments to evaluate the effectiveness of new strategies in developing the global competence of prospective teachers. (Longview Foundation 2008, p. 6)

Discussing the policy implications of that report, Professor Yong Zhao, one of the members of the expert group convened by the Longview Foundation, explains how current policies for teacher education in the United States are in fact barriers to achieving the recommendations of the report (Zhao 2010).

With respect to ongoing professional development, the findings from our recent cross-national study of effective professional development programs focused on educating the whole child provide the following guidance (Reimers 2018):

1. Design programs that are responsive to the needs of teachers and to the context in which they teach. For example, the cycle of whole school improvement proposed in the book Empowering Students to Improve the World in Sixty Lessons does that by situating professional development in the school and by engaging teachers themselves in defining professional development needs based on their proposed approach to global education.
2. Create multiple and intensive opportunities to build capacities, over an entire school year, or more.
3. Rely on a variety of modalities of professional development: independent study, discussions in professional communities with peers, coaching, demonstrations, independent research projects, and reflection on action. Access to exemplars can be a valuable resource to help teachers develop their own improvement goals. For instance, the partnership for twenty-first-century skills, an advocacy organization in the United States, has curated a series of exemplars of twenty-first-century schools which can be studied by in-service teachers (Battelle for Kids 2019). The World Economic Forum has provided mini cases of education programs which exemplify how to cultivate the capacities necessary for the fourth industrial revolution, including global citizenship skills (World Economic Forum 2020). In addition, study abroad programs can help in-service teachers develop their own intercultural competence and global knowledge. A study of the impact of a short-term study abroad program for in-service teachers designed a program integrating the five elements which existing research underscores as critical: the value of cultural immersion experiences, opportunities to teach, opportunities to learn the language, reflection, and collaboration. The study included only 12 participants, and found relatively more gains in knowledge about the culture than about intercultural attitudes and skills (He et al. 2017, p. 148).
4. The goals of these programs should be to help teachers develop a blend of capacities, including specific teaching techniques, approaches, and conceptual understanding.
5. Support teacher development in cognitive and socio-emotional domains.
6. Provide examples of instruction and assessment in global education.
7. Create multiple learning opportunities embedded in the school context.
8. Build partnerships with other organizations, such as universities and NGOs, which can enhance the capacity of the school. An immediate way to augment the capacity of the school is to tap into the community of parents as a resource. The World Course creates multiple opportunities for parents to serve as resources

6.5 Staff and Development

for the curriculum. There are also a number of organizations which can augment the school capacity, for instance offering professional development or support or both. For example, i-Earn is an organization that helps teachers connect with colleagues interested in developing collaborative projects between their students and students in other countries. As the program i-Earn supports teachers in developing those collaborations, the experience itself is a form of professional development for the participating teachers. A study of 126 teachers in the International Baccalaureate program in over 30 countries participating in online discussion forums found that teachers gained new understandings about open-mindedness, interconnectedness and cross-cultural learning from these exchanges (Harshman and Augustine 2013). The British Council Connecting Classrooms has similar purposes. Empatico is an organization that also helps teachers find colleagues across the world for collaborations of shorter duration than the project-based initiatives that i-Earn supports. The global classroom project also helps educators find partners to collaborate on teaching projects.

There are many other organizations that can offer similar forms of support. For example, Facing History and Ourselves is an organization that offers teacher professional development to teach history, Holocaust studies and civics. The Global Scholars Program at Bloomberg's Philanthropies provides teachers with curriculum and professional development to teach about global themes, with colleagues in several cities around the world. Education First is an organization that works with public schools organizing short-term study abroad for students, those visits often involve teachers and collaborations to integrate the short trips with longer periods of study during the academic year. Envoys works with teachers developing customized global curriculum that includes a study abroad experience for students. World Savvy supports teachers developing global curriculum.

9. Favor whole-school approaches to professional development over the development of selected individual teachers.
10. Use measurement to gain formative feedback that can be used in professional development. The role of assessment has been discussed previously.
11. Structure professional development to help the school become a "learning organization," a theme developed in the next section.

6.6 School Organization

The work of teachers and students does not take place in a vacuum, but is nested in organizations whose characteristics and processes shape their interactions. An important feature of schools' organization is governance and leadership: what kind of decisions are made at the school level and how the school is led. Over the last several years, a consensus has emerged in favor of more school autonomy for decisions where those closer to students are best positioned to have the necessary knowledge to make them. Along with this view, ideas about leadership as a distributed enterprise among those in the school have also emerged. These views reflect an evolving intellectual tradition that sees schools as learning organizations. The intellectual foundation of that tradition is in the field of organizational studies. The term "learning organization" itself originates in the theory of systems thinking developed by von Bertalanffy (1938). The theory of learning organizations was developed by Argyris and Schon (1978), Senge et al. (1990) and others. Several authors extended the use of the concept of learning organizations to the study of schools in ways that have become widely accepted when thinking about school change (Senge et al. 2000; Fullan 1995, 2001; Hargreaves and Fullan 2012; Bryk and Scheider 2002). A recent review of the scholarship on schools as learning organizations (Kools and Stoll 2017, pp. 61–63) synthesizes that literature in seven dimensions:

Developing a shared vision centered on the learning of all students
Creating and supporting continuous professional learning for all staff
Promoting team learning and collaboration among staff
Establishing a culture of inquiry, exploration, and innovation
Embedding systems for collecting and exchanging knowledge and learning
Learning with and from the external environment and larger system
Modeling and growing learning leadership

These dimensions are readily applicable to thinking about supporting global education, as I have observed in my work with schools and networks using the approach to change presented in *Empowering Students to Improve the World in Sixty Lessons*. The thirteen-step protocol guides professional communities in school in a collaborative process that includes negotiating a long term vision, translating it into a specific competency framework, examining the work already going on in the school in light of this framework, deciding on a next step for improvement, communicating in dialogue with the extended school community, deciding, obtaining resources, developing a framework to monitor implementation, developing a communication and a professional development strategy, executing, evaluating, and iterating (Reimers et al. 2017).

Developing a shared vision centered on the learning of all students requires creating opportunities for global education not just for some students, but for all. It is often the case that schools offer some opportunities to support global education for students in the form of foreign language courses, or courses on world history or geography, or study abroad, or opportunities to engage in global projects, but these activities are optional and can in practice be accessed only by a small fraction of the student body. A challenge of an inclusive and capacious vision for global education is to create conditions that ensure these opportunities for all students. For instance, if a key component of a school program of global education involves foreign travel for students, and this travel is funded by parents, an obvious limitation of that strategy is that it is likely to exclude those students whose parents cannot afford the cost of travel. Similarly, curricular choices can favor some students at the expense of others. For example, one of the approaches used to advance global education consists of creating certificates of global competency that recognize students for engaging in a range of these activities over the course of their studies. A study of the implementation of global education in two high schools in Massachusetts found two approaches had been used to advance a global education program. One of them relied on infusing global connections in the curriculum of all subjects, while the other relied on certificates as a way to allow students to build a personalized global education program. Many teachers expressed concern that the certificates provided opportunities to an elite group of students, leaving out most students:

> [All participants interviewed] referred to the development and implementation of a student-centered, self-selecting Global Competence Program (GCP). The purpose of the GCP is to allow students to build a portfolio of courses, travel experiences, and community service requirements geared toward the acquisition of knowledge and skills that will in turn prepare them for success in a global society. The students submit a completed portfolio, and if accepted, are awarded a certificate of global competence at the time of graduation. (Kilpatrick 2010, p. 99)

The dimension of creating and supporting continuous professional learning for all staff is enacted in establishing a process of change at the school level which embeds learning in the process of doing the work. In effect, the thirteen steps are a protocol to establish and support a professional learning community of global education, enhanced with participation in a network of schools pursuing similar aspirations.

Promoting team learning and collaboration is reflected in the very design of the thirteen steps as an activity dependent upon distributed leadership. The process outlined in the protocol relies on a culture of inquiry and exploration, as it frames the process as experimenting in order to test the two hypotheses implicit in all curriculum: if we teach A then students will learn B, and if students learn B then outcomes C, D, and E will be achieved. The design of a process as one of continuous improvement, relying on design thinking methodologies to develop and test a global education prototype, reflects the idea that global education is a process of continuous experimentation and learning.

Embedding systems to collect and exchange knowledge and learning is reflected in the idea that theories of action about global education are evaluated, as is the impact of professional development.

The dimension of learning with and from the external environment and the larger system is reflected in establishing partnerships with other institutions, such as universities and community resources, as a way to provide access to knowledge and augment the capacity of the school. Many universities have developed resources and can support schools in developing curriculum and offering opportunities for teacher professional development. In the United States, for instance, grants from the federal government support centers for international studies, most of which have an outreach requirement to collaborate with schools or with other institutions that reach the public (National Research Council 2007).

The dimension of modeling and growing learning leadership is reflected in the distributed leadership of this process, and in engaging students in leadership roles in constructing projects and other opportunities for global education.

References

Alberta Council for Environmental Education. (2017). *What is excellent climate change education?* Canada: Alberta.

Argyris, C., & Schon, D. (1978). *Organizational learning: A theory of action perspective.* Mass and Reading: Addison Wesley.

Asia Society. (2019). *Global competence outcomes and rubrics.* Center for Global Education. Retrieved from https://asiasociety.org/education/global-competence-outcomes-and-rubrics.

Aspen Institute. (2019). *From a nation at risk to a nation at Hope.* National Commission on Social, Emotional and Academic Development. Retrieved from https://www.aspeninstitute.org/programs/national-commission-on-social-emotional-and-academic-development/.

Australian Curriculum. (2019). *Cross-curricular priorities.* Retrieved from https://www.australiancurriculum.edu.au/f-10-curriculum/cross-curriculum-priorities/.

Battelle for Kids. (2019). *21st century learning exemplars.* Retrieved from http://www.battelleforkids.org/networks/p21/21st-century-learning-exemplar-program.

Beltramo, L., & Duncheon, J. (2013). Globalization standards: A comparison of U.S. and non-U.S. social studies curricula. *The Journal of Social Studies Research, 37*(2), 97–109.

Bertalanffy, L. (1938). A quantitative theory of organic growth. *Human Biology, 10,* 181–213.

Boix Mansilla, V. (2013). *Internal working paper: Longview Foundation interim report, Project Zero.* Cambridge, MA: Harvard Graduate School of Education.

Boix Mansilla, V., & Jackson, A. (2011) *Educating for global competence. Preparing our youth to engage the world.* Washington, DC: Asia Society. Retrieved from https://asiasociety.org/files/book-globalcompetence.pdf.

Boynton-Hauwerwas, L., Skawinski, S., & Ryan, L. (2017). The longitudinal impact of teaching abroad: An analysis of intercultural development. *Teaching and Teacher Education, 67,* 202–213.

Bryk, A., & Schneider, B. (2002). *Trust in schools: A core resource for school improvement.* New York: Russell Sage.

Bryk, A., Gomez, L., Grunow, A., & LeMahieu, P. (2015). *Learning to improve: How America's schools can get better at getting better.* Cambridge, MA: Harvard Education Publishing.

Center for Universal Education at Brookings. (2017). *Measuring Global Citizenship Education. A Collection of Practices and Tools.* Washington, DC: Brookings Institution. https://www.brookings.edu/wp-content/uploads/2017/04/global_20170411_measuring-global-citizenship.pdf

Chen, G. (2017). Climate change to become part of core curriculum in public schools. *Public School Review.* Retrieved from https://www.publicschoolreview.com/blog/climate-change-to-become-part-of-core-curriculum-in-public-schools.

Commonwealth of Australia. (2012). *Teacher Resources to Encourage a global perspective across the curriculum.* Education Services Australia, Global Education Project, Global Education. Retrieved from https://www.globaleducation.edu.au/teaching-and-learning/australian-curriculum.html.

Danish Institute for Human Rights. (2014). *Mapping of human rights education in Danish schools.* Copenhagen: Danish Institute for Human Rights.

Doppen, F., & An, J. (2014). Student teaching abroad: Enhancing global awareness. *International Education, 43*(2), 59–75.

Education Services Australia. (2019). *Teaching strategies.* Retrieved from https://www.globaleducation.edu.au/teaching-and-learning/teaching-strategies.html.

Facing History and Ourselves. (2019). *Educator resources.* Retrieved from https://www.facinghistory.org/educator-resources.

Fullan, M. (1995). The school as a learning organization: Distant dreams. *Theory Into Practice, 34*(4), 230–235.

Fullan, M. (2001). *The new meaning of educational change.* New York: Teachers College Press.

Gapminder. (2013). *The ignorance survey: United States.* Retrieved from https://static.gapminder.org/GapminderMedia/wp-uploads/Results-from-the-Ignorance-Survey-in-the-US.pdf.

References

Haass, R. (2020). *The World. A Brief Introduction*. New York. Penguin Press.

Hargreaves, A., & Fullan, M. (2012). *Professional capital*. New York: Teachers College Press.

Harshman, J., & Augustine, T. (2013). Fostering global citizenship education for teachers through online research. *The Educational Forum, 77*(4), 450–463.

He, Y., Lungren, K., & Pynes, P. (2017). Impact of short-term study abroad program: Inservice teachers' development of intercultural competence and pedagogical beliefs. *Teaching and Teacher Education, 66,* 147–157.

High Resolves. (2019). Retrieved from https://highresolves.org/.

Kerkhoff, S. (2017). Designing global futures: A mixed methods study to develop and validate the teaching for global readiness scale. *Teaching and Teacher Education, 65,* 91–106.

Kilpatrick, J. (2010). *Global education in Massachusetts: A case study of two high schools*. Doctoral Dissertation. Boston University.

Klein, J. (2017). *Global education guidebook: Humanizing K-12 classrooms worldwide through equitable partnerships (How to promote multicultural education and nurture global citizens)*. Bloomington, IN: Solution Tree Press.

Kools, M., & Stoll, L. (2017). *What makes a school a learning organization. OECD. Directorate of Education and Skills*. Education Working Paper No. 137. Paris: OECD.

Lee, J. (2011). International field experience. What do student teachers learn? *Australian Journal of Teacher Education, 36*(10). Retrieved from https://ro.ecu.edu.au/ajte/vol36/iss10/1/.

Longview Foundation. (2008). *Teacher preparation for the global age*. Silver Spring, MD: Longview Foundation.

McKeown, R., & Hopkins, C. (2014). *Education for sustainable development in teacher education*. Paris: UNESCO.

Merryfield, M. M. (1998). Pedagogy for global perspectives in education: Studies of teachers' thinking and practice. *Theory & Research in Social Education, 26*(3), 342–379.

Modern Language Association. (2019). *Report from the MLA ad-hoc committee on teaching*. Retrieved from https://www.mla.org/Resources/Research/Surveys-Reports-and-Other-Documents/Teaching-Enrollments-and-Programs/Report-from-the-MLA-Ad-Hoc-Committee-on-Teaching/Read-the-Report-Online.

Mundy, K., & Manion, C. (2008). Global education in Canadian elementary schools: An exploratory study. *Canadian Journal of Education, 31*(4), 941–974.

Myers, J. (2006). Rethinking the social studies curriculum in the context of globalization: Education for global citizenship in the U.S. *Theory and Research in Social Education, 34*(3), 370–394.

National Research Council. (2007). *International education and Foreign languages: Keys to securing America's future*. Washington, DC: The National Academies Press.

North Carolina Department of Public Instruction. (2017). *NC global ready district. Implementation plan*. Retrieved from http://www.ncpublicschools.org/docs/globaled/actions/district-rubric.pdf.

North Carolina State Board of Education. (2013). *Preparing students for the world: Final report of the State Board of Education's task force on global education*. Retrieved from http://www.ncpublicschools.org/globaled/.

OECD. (2012). *How green are today's 15 year olds. In focus*. https://www.oecd.org/pisa/pisaproducts/pisainfocus/50150271.pdf Accessed March 13, 2020.

OECD. (2019a). *TALIS 2018 results. Volume I. Teachers and school leaders as lifelong learners*. Retrieved December 3, 2019, from http://www.oecd.org/education/talis/.

OECD. (2019b). *PISA 2018 results. What students know and can do* (Vol. 1). Retrieved December 6, 2019, from https://www.oecd.org/pisa/.

OECD and Asia Society. (2018). *Teaching for global competence in a rapidly changing world*. Paris: OECD.

Pellegrino, J. W., & Hilton, M. L. (Eds.). (2012). *Education for life and work: Developing transferable knowledge and skills in the 21st century*. Washington, DC: The National Academies Press.

Peterson, A., Milligan, A., & Wood, B. (2018). Global citizenship education in Australasia. In I. Davies, et al. (Eds.), *The Palgrave handbook of global citizenship and education*. London: Palgrave-Macmillan.

Poole, C. (2014). *Global perspectives of pre-service teachers: A comparative study*. Doctoral Dissertation, University of Central Florida, College of Education. Retrieved from https://stars.library.ucf.edu/etd/4550/.

Rapoport, A. (2010). We cannot teach what we don't know: Indiana teachers talk about global citizenship education. *Education, Citizenship and Social Justice, 5*(3), 179–190.

Reimers, F., et al. (2018). *Learning to collaborate for the global common good*. Charleston, SC: CreateSpace

Reimers, F. (2020a, In Press). *Audacious education purposes*. Springer.

Reimers, F. (2020b, In Press). *Empowering teachers to build a better world*. Springer.

Reimers, F., & Chung, K. (Eds.). (2018). *Preparing teachers to educate whole students: An international comparative study*. Cambridge, MA: Harvard Education Publishing.

Reimers, F., Chopra, V., Chung, C., Higdon, J., & O'Donnell, E. B. (2016). *Empowering global citizens*. Charleston, SC: CreateSpace.

Reimers, F., et al. (2017). *Empowering students to improve the world in sixty lessons*. Charleston, SC: CreateSpace.

Robbins, M., Francis, L., & Elliott, E. (2003). Attitudes towards education for global citizenship among trainee teachers. *Research in Education, 69*(1), 93–98.

Senge, P., et al. (1990). *The fifth discipline: The art and practice of the learning organization*. New York: Doubleday.

Senge, P., et al. (2000). *Schools that learn: A fifth discipline fieldbook for educators, parents, and everyone who cares about education*. New York: Doubleday.

Smith, T. (2014). Incorporating global projects into teacher education: A look at practices and perceptions of pre-service and mentor teachers. *Global Partners in Education Journal, 4*(1), 41–63.

Southern Poverty Law Center. (2019). *Hate at school*. Retrieved from https://www.splcenter.org/sites/default/files/tt_2019_hate_at_school_report_final_0.pdf.

Tichnor-Wagner, A., Parkhouse, H., Glazier, J., & Cain, J. M. (2016). Expanding approaches to teaching for diversity and social justice in K-12 education: Fostering global citizenship across the content areas. *Education Policy Analysis Archives, 24*(59).

UNESCO. (1994). Salamanca statement on principles, policies and practice in special needs education. In *World conference on special needs education: Access and quality*, 7–10 June 1994. Paris: UNESCO.

UNESCO. (2012). *Education sector responses to climate change*. Bangkok: UNESCO.

UNESCO. (2017). *Education for people and planet*. Global Education Monitoring Report. Paris: UNESCO.

UNESCO. (2018). *Progress on education for sustainable development and global citizenship education: Findings of the 6th consultation on the implementation of the 1974 recommendation concerning education for international understanding*. Retrieved January 23, 2020, from https://unesdoc.unesco.org/ark:/48223/pf0000266176.

UNESCO. (2019a). *Global citizenship education*. Retrieved from https://en.unesco.org/themes/gced.

UNESCO. (2019b). *Education for sustainable development*. Retrieved January 23, 2020, from https://en.unesco.org/themes/education-sustainable-development.

United Nations. (2020). *Sustainable development goals*. Retrieved January 23, 2020, from https://www.un.org/sustainabledevelopment/education/.

United States Department of Education. (2017). *Framework for developing global and cultural competencies to advance equity, excellence and economic competitiveness*. Retrieved from https://sites.ed.gov/international/global-and-cultural-competency/.

Utah State Board of Education. (2019). *Welcome to dual language immersion*. Retrieved from https://www.schools.utah.gov/curr/dualimmersion.

References

Van Werven, I. (2012). *Global citizenship at teacher training colleges in Gelderland, the Netherlands*. Masters Thesis, Wageningen University, Department of Social Sciences Rural Development Sociology. http://edepot.wur.nl/202782.

Vansteenkiste, M., & Sheldon, K. (2006). There's nothing more practical than a good theory: Integrating motivational interviewing and self-determination theory. *British Journal of Clinical Psychology,* (45), 63–82. The British Psychological Society.

West, M. (2007). *Testing, learning, and teaching: The effects of test-based accountability on student achievement and instructional time in core academic subjects*. In E. Chester, D. Ravitch, B. Thomas (Eds.), *Beyond the Basics: Achieving a Liberal Education for All Children Finn* Fordham Institute. Pages 45–61.

World Bank. (2019). *Equity and inclusion in education in world bank projects: Persons with disabilities, indigenous peoples, and sexual and gender minorities*. Washington, DC: World Bank Group.

World Economic Forum. (2020). Schools of the future: Defining new models of education for the fourth industrial revolution. https://www.weforum.org/reports/schools-of-the-future-defining-new-models-of-education-for-the-fourth-industrial-revolution. Accessed March 13, 2020

Zhao, Y. (2010). Preparing globally competent teachers: A new imperative for teacher education. *Journal of Teacher Education, 61*(5), 422–431.

Open Access This chapter is licensed under the terms of the Creative Commons Attribution 4.0 International License (http://creativecommons.org/licenses/by/4.0/), which permits use, sharing, adaptation, distribution and reproduction in any medium or format, as long as you give appropriate credit to the original author(s) and the source, provide a link to the Creative Commons license and indicate if changes were made.

The images or other third party material in this chapter are included in the chapter's Creative Commons license, unless indicated otherwise in a credit line to the material. If material is not included in the chapter's Creative Commons license and your intended use is not permitted by statutory regulation or exceeds the permitted use, you will need to obtain permission directly from the copyright holder.

Chapter 7
A Political Perspective and Global Education

Because schools and education systems affect many different stakeholders, it is to be expected that the interests of those stakeholders should be crucial to the fate of any efforts of educational change. The two obvious implications of this truism are that the first step in designing a program of global education is understanding how key stakeholder groups are positioned vis-a-vis the program. The second implication is that a political strategy to implement change requires mobilizing as much support as possible and demobilizing detractors. Collaborative negotiating strategies can help widen the support for a program. In a recent compilation of reflections of former ministers of education and other education leaders on their own efforts to produce large scale change most made reference to how crucial the politics of the process of policy design and implementation were to reform (Reimers 2019).

In the United States, for example, analysis of history textbooks shows that publishing companies distribute different versions of the same history books in ways which are responsive to prevailing political views of the school boards in various states. As a result, history is taught in a way that reflects the existing political divides in the country, reproducing such divides. For instance, gun regulation is a divisive issue in American politics, whereas textbooks in California include information about the rulings on the Second Amendment to the US Constitution which have allowed for some gun regulation, textbooks in California omit this information (Goldstein 2020).

Similarly, the politicization of discussions of climate change leads teachers to teach content which deviates from the scientific consensus. A recent study of the National Center for Science Education of how teachers teach climate change in the US found that while three-quarters of the science teachers did address climate change in the curriculum, only 54% did so in ways which were aligned with the scientific consensus, whereas 10% taught incorrect knowledge, such as the ideas that recent increases in temperature are due to natural causes and to teach that it is not the case that the scientific consensus that recent global warming is primarily being caused by human release of greenhouse gases from fossil fuels; an additional 31% of the teachers sent mixed messages in their teaching, correctly teaching that the scientific consensus that recent global warming is primarily being caused by human release of greenhouse gases from fossil fuels, but incorrectly teaching that many scientists believe that recent increases in temperature are likely due to natural causes (Plutzer et al. 2016, 16).

Tools like political mapping can be helpful in identifying and determining the interests of key stakeholder groups, and in guiding a process of coalition building, negotiation, and mobilization in favor of change. Communications is an indispensable element of a change process, as is viewing the process of designing a global education program as a negotiation that attempts to reconcile as many interests of key stakeholder groups as possible. This is the reason beginning where people are makes for good politics, as does using participatory approaches that allow various stakeholder groups to bring their interests to the process of developing a global education program. Sometimes opposition to global education change reflects lack of clarity or misinterpretation about what is expected. I have found that providing opportunities for teams to collaborate in the design of curriculum and actual lesson plans can facilitate communication, clarify misconceptions, and provide opportunities to productively negotiate various perspectives.

A study of two district-based programs of global education in North Carolina found that both relied on strong support from district leadership, including the superintendent, from communication, engagement, and mobilization of school board members, school administrators, teachers, and community members, including stakeholders planning the initiatives, and building pockets of success (Tichnor–Wagner 2019).

However, there may be limits to what inclusion, participation, and communication can deliver as there may be genuine interests that diverge with global education. An emerging populist nationalism, with strong xenophobic undertones, is creating veritable divides within many societies, between those who see themselves as part of a global community, with shared responsibility to address some of these challenges, and those who do not see themselves as global citizens. A survey administered by the Globescan-BBC in 2016 in a range of countries[1] shows that while the percentage of the population that sees themselves as global citizens is growing over time, there are clear splits in the population in most countries in this respect. On average, 22% of the population strongly agrees with the statement that they see themselves more as a global citizen than as a citizen of their own country, and an additional 29% agree with the statement. On the other hand, 20% strongly disagree with the statement, and an additional 23% disagree. The population is, therefore, split in the middle, with half of the population divided between two extreme views (Globescan-BBC 2016).

There are also differences among countries in the percentage of the population that sees themselves as global citizens. Whereas those who strongly agree or agree with the statement that they see themselves more as global citizens than as citizens of their own country represent 45% in Spain, 35% in Greece, 39% Nigeria, and over 20% in Canada, the US, the UK, Peru, Brazil, Kenya, Ghana, China, India, Pakistan;

---

[1] The survey was administered in Canada, United States of America, Peru, Brazil, Mexico, Chile, Spain, Greece, United Kingdom, Germany, Russia, Nigeria, Kenya, Ghana, China, India, Pakistan and Indonesia.

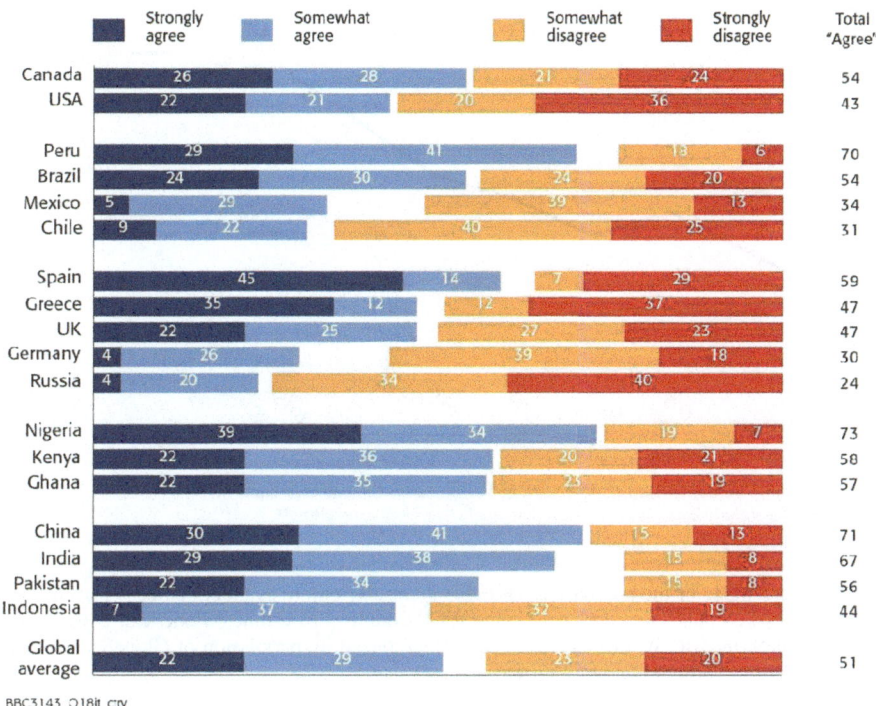

Fig. 7.1 Percentage of the population who sees themselves more as global citizens than as citizens of their own country in several countries in 2016 (Globescan-BBC 2016) *Source* GlobeScan/BBC World Service Poll (2016). Reproduced by permission of GlobeScan for the GlobeScan/BBC World Service Poll (2016)

in contrast, less than 10% of the population agrees with that statement in Mexico, Chile, Germany, Russia, and Indonesia (Globescan-BBC 2016) (Fig. 7.1).

The percentage of the population who sees themselves more as global citizens than as citizens of their own country has increased considerably in Non-OECD countries, from 44% in 2001 to 56% in 2016, but has declined slightly in OECD countries, from 44% to 42% during the same period (GlobeScan-BBC 2016) (Fig. 7.2).

Some of the developments characterizing globalization, particularly in the area of communication technology, are enabling individuals to organize in unprecedented ways. This includes those with intolerant views and hate groups. It is also possible for various organizations, or states, to spread misinformation, creating "echo chambers" in which "alternative facts" are given the same credence as the truth. For

I See Myself More as a Global Citizen than a Citizen of My Country
"Agree,"* OECD vs Non-OECD Countries,** Trends, 2001–2016

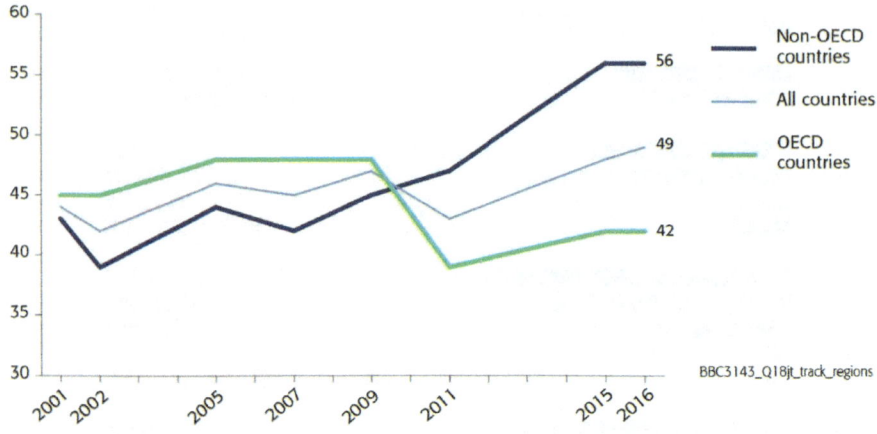

*"Strongly agree" plus "Somewhat agree"
**OECD countries include Canada, Chile, Germany, Mexico, Spain, UK, and USA; Non-OECD countries include Brazil, China, India, Indonesia, Kenya, Nigeria, and Russia.
Not all countries were asked in all years.

Fig. 7.2 Percentage of the population who sees themselves more as global citizens than as citizens of their own country in OECD and non-OECD countries over time (GlobeScan-BBC 2016). *Source* GlobeScan/BBC World Service (2016). Reproduced by permission of GlobeScan for the GlobeScan/BBC World Service Poll (2016)

example, there is emerging evidence that groups with ties to the Russian government are using social networking sites as tools to viralize information that creates racial discord and anti-immigrant sentiments in the United States (Becker 2019). Two independent reports commissioned by the US Senate demonstrate that Russian agents used social media to exacerbate racial tensions in the United States and to discourage African Americans from participating in the 2016 election (Howard et al. 2019; DiResta et al. 2019). Participation in extremely intolerant groups (hate groups or white supremacist) is increasing in some countries. In the United States, the Federal Bureau of Investigation has reported an increase in the number of reported hate crimes in recent years (a 17% increase in 2017). The most common bias categories focus on race/ethnicity/ancestry (60%), religion (21%) and sexual orientation (16%) (FBI 2017). This climate can clearly influence local communities and their support for global education.

Contention with respect to global education stems also from other priorities for schools. State mandates and state-mandated assessments reflect the prevailing views of the most powerful groups with respect to what should be emphasized in schools. Those standards and assessments are important, a reason to see them as a lever to advance global education. When they don't do so explicitly, global education needs to be negotiated within the context of those standards. A study of the implementation of a global education program in two high schools in Massachusetts found that in an urban high school, the pressure to focus on state mandates competed with the desire to implement the program of global education:

> Four teachers, including one who is also a parent, noted that while the richness of the urban high school provides students with an opportunity to be exposed to multiple perspectives and experiences, the focus on achievement in the area of basic skills remains the most important priority (Kilpatrick 2010, p. 194).

> While teachers acknowledged the pressure created by the tests, particularly in the urban school, they were nonetheless supportive of them because they believed they had helped raise standards in the school. Administrators thought teachers should find a way to infuse global education within the existing standards and curriculum, even though opportunities to develop the capacity to do this were absent (Ibid, p. 200–201).

The politics of global education need not be all politics involving governments. Civil society organizations can play an important role in favor, as well as against, global education. A study of programs of professional development building the capacity of teachers to educate the whole child found that civil society organizations had the capacity to provide continuity and support, overcoming the cycles of intermittent support from government (Reimers 2018). In the United States, for example, the Asia Society has played an important role over many years supporting global education through a variety of programs, including a network to support internationally themed high schools, a program to recognize effective global education practices, and a program of publications that has produced standards, frameworks, and exemplars of good practice.

In Australia, the Australian Association for Environmental Education lobbied the Federal Government to educate effectively about climate change, which resulted in the creation of an Education for Sustainable Development program, which included curriculum and block grants to help reduce the carbon footprint of schools (UNESCO 2012, p. 13).

Similarly, professional organizations can provide support for global education. The association of social studies teachers in the United States has contributed to shape an understanding within the profession of the importance of teaching American history in the context of global events.

The Massachusetts Association of School Superintendents lobbied the state with partial success for more attention to global education in 2009, advocating for dedicated attention to global studies in the Department of Education, educating the public about global education, and funding the education and foreign language fund.

International governmental and non-governmental organizations can also provide support to government and groups advancing global education, demonstrating the cosmopolitan nature of the global education movement. The United Nations and UNESCO, for example, were created to advance human rights, and have made global education one of their longstanding priorities since the Universal Declaration was adopted in 1948 and since UNESCO was created in 1945. A cornerstone of that global advocacy is "The International Recommendation concerning Education for International Understanding, Cooperation and Peace and Education relating to Human Rights and Fundamental Freedoms", adopted by member states at

UNESCOs 18th session in 1974, which recommends that member states teach peace, human rights, international understanding, tolerance, and other humanistic values (UNESCO 1974). In the United Kingdom, Oxfam played a crucial role in advancing global citizenship curriculum, developing curriculum and advocating its adoption.

The Council of Europe Charter on Education for Democratic Citizenship and Human Rights Education was adopted by 50 countries in 2010. Two years later 90% of the countries reported that they were promoting democratic governance through participation of students and parents in school decision-making (UNESCO 2017, p. 294).

References

Becker, J. (2019, August 11). How nationalism found a home in Sweden. *New York Times*.
DiResta, R. et al. (2019). *The tactics and trops of the internet research agency. New knowledge, Columbia university and canfield research*. https://disinformationreport.blob.core.windows.net/disinformation-report/NewKnowledge-Disinformation-Report-Whitepaper.pdf.
Federal Bureau of Investigation. (2017). *Hate crime statistics*. https://ucr.fbi.gov/hate-crime/2017.
Globescan-BBC World Service Poll. (2016). *Global citizenship a growing sentiment among citizens of emerging economies*. https://globescan.com/wp-content/uploads/2016/04/BBC_GlobeScan_Identity_Season_Press_Release_April%2026.pdf.
Goldstein, D. (2020, January 12). Two states. Eight textbooks. Two American stories. *The New York Times*.
Howard, P. et al. (2019). *The IRA, social media and political polarization in the United States, 2012–2018*. University of Oxford and Graphika. https://comprop.oii.ox.ac.uk/research/ira-political-polarization/.
Kilpatrick, J. (2010). *Global education in massachusetts: A case study of two high schools*. Doctoral Dissertation. Boston University.
Plutzer, E., Hannah, A. L., Rosenau, J., McCaffrey, M., Berbeco, M., & Reid, A. H. (2016). Mixed Messages: How climate is taught in America's schools. Oakland, CA: National Center for Science Education. http://ncse.com/files/MixedMessages.pdf.
Reimers, F. (2018). A study in how teachers learn to educate whole students and how schools build the capacity to support them. In F. Reimers & K. Chung (Eds.), *Preparing teachers to educate whole students. An international comparative study* (pp. 1–32.). Cambridge, MA: Harvard Education Publishing.
Reimers, F. (Ed.). (2019). *Letters to a new minister of education*. Middletown, DE: Kindle Direct Publishing.
Tichnor-Wagner, A. (2019, July 24). District agency in implementing instructional reform: a comparative case study of global education. *Journal of Educational Change*.
UNESCO. (2012). *Education sector responses to climate change*. Bangkok: Unesco.
UNESCO. (1974). *Recommendation concerning education for international understanding, co-operation and peace and education relating to human rights and fundamental freedoms*. http://portal.unesco.org/en/ev.php-URL_ID=13088&URL_DO=DO_TOPIC&URL_SECTION=201.html.
UNESCO. (2017). *Education for people and planet. Global education monitoring report*. Paris: Unesco.

Open Access This chapter is licensed under the terms of the Creative Commons Attribution 4.0 International License (http://creativecommons.org/licenses/by/4.0/), which permits use, sharing, adaptation, distribution and reproduction in any medium or format, as long as you give appropriate credit to the original author(s) and the source, provide a link to the Creative Commons license and indicate if changes were made.

The images or other third party material in this chapter are included in the chapter's Creative Commons license, unless indicated otherwise in a credit line to the material. If material is not included in the chapter's Creative Commons license and your intended use is not permitted by statutory regulation or exceeds the permitted use, you will need to obtain permission directly from the copyright holder.

Chapter 8
Conclusions. Integrating the Five Perspectives

There is no more important challenge facing the world than educating the next generation so that they have the competencies to invent their future. This will include being able to address the challenges we are passing on to them: environmental degradation, social exclusion, and the various forms of violence, within and across nations, that undermine the possibility that we can live in peace.

Three centuries ago, during the long eighteenth century, a powerful set of ideas transformed humanity. The Enlightenment put forth the audacious proposition that ordinary people could rule themselves, and improve their lives individually and collectively, as a result of the use of reason. The age of reason gave us three institutions, joined at the hip: democracy, public education, and the modern research university. Like the Enlightenment itself, these institutions reflect a cosmopolitan ambition, the ambition to improve the human condition through collaboration, including collaboration across borders.

Out of this global project of collective self-improvement was born public education. An institution designed to develop human capacities for self-rule and for societal improvement. It was only in the last century that most of the world's children gained access to school, as a result of the inclusion of the right to education in the Universal Declaration of Human Rights, and as a result of the leadership and collaborations made possible by the creation of the United Nations and UNESCO. These institutions made the goal of educating all of the world's children a truly cosmopolitan project, both in the processes they created and supported to accelerate cross-national exchanges to educate all children, and in their advocacy for the purposes of education to develop true cosmopolitan global citizens.

As the world around us changes with accelerating speed, we stand at a moment of extraordinary possibilities created by the social, political, and technological developments of the last century. However, we also face challenges that are daunting and deeply consequential for our very survival as a species. We are at a moment of choice as to how we are to face those challenges.

Due to the success of the enterprise of providing access to education for all we are ready, like never before, to equip all children and youth with the capabilities to help them make the best possible choices. To do this, however, it is essential that schools, this wonderful invention to make the world better, take on directly the task of engaging students with the challenges the world faces.

Preparing students to understand those challenges, to care about them and to gain the skills to address them is the most important leadership task that teachers and school leaders face. Facing it will require advancing global education in our schools. Global education is not a new fad, a small tweak, another addition in the large menu in the cafeteria that curriculum has become in many schools. Global education is an approach to reorient the entire enterprise of how students learn and teachers teach. It may involve additions to the curriculum, but it first involves intentionally examining and revising the existing curriculum, pedagogy and school organization so that they stand the best chance of helping students understand the world and figuring out how to make it better.

Ideas about how to make education global have been around for some time. In many ways, the institution of public education is already global in that it exists all over the world, includes most children and there are remarkable similarities in how schools are configured globally. But as the world in which we live changes rapidly, our schools have not yet reached their potential to truly prepare all children to be ready for those changes. This has not been for lack of trying, but for a limited way of thinking about how to bring this change about. Global education has been, for too long, a domain for the initiated, a conversation among specialists, largely academics, who have spent much energy and ink deliberating what global education is. These debates, valuable as they are, have had the unfortunate effect of causing a certain amount of confusion among practitioners and the public. Not because teachers and parents cannot engage and even enjoy discussions at thirty thousand feet from the classroom, but because the conversations have been too disconnected from that domain where education takes place every day.

If global education is to seize its potential to make schools more relevant, it must include practitioners in the task of inventing it. Such invention is not just about the theoretical discussion of what a global citizen or a good society is, it is especially about how we can do this work with our students, in our school, next Monday morning. Implementation of global education cannot be an afterthought to theoretical debates, it must be part and parcel of the debates.

Leading a process that makes such deep change possible in schools can be aided by thinking about change through five complementary perspectives. One is a cultural perspective: what is it that society expects of schools and what are the social imperatives of our times? The second is a psychological perspective: what do we know about how children and adults learn, and how do we reconcile the normative imperatives that a cultural perspective offers, with the scientific knowledge about how to structure the most effective learning opportunities for students? The third is a professional perspective: how do we approach the task of making schools more relevant in a way that depends on expert knowledge and on the best use of reason to guide practice? How can a reorientation of education to make it more global serve also as an avenue to make education more professional, while depending on the professionalism already existing in the enterprise? The fourth is an institutional perspective: how do we align the various elements of the system of education so

8 Conclusions. Integrating the Five Perspectives

that, together, they all support forms of teaching and learning that truly empower students to understand and improve the world? The fifth is a political perspective: how do we make the best of the reality that schools touch many different interests, and align those interests on behalf of an education that advances the global project of collective self-improvement it was created to advance?

Each of these frames is complementary to the others. Not only does each one shed light on important elements that must be addressed in a change process, but using them in combination can help lead change more capaciously. It is in the interaction of the activities animated by simultaneous attention to the five frames that global education can reach levels of impact not yet reached in most schools.

I hope the ideas presented in this book inspire your efforts to make schools more relevant, so our students can build a better world.

Open Access This chapter is licensed under the terms of the Creative Commons Attribution 4.0 International License (http://creativecommons.org/licenses/by/4.0/), which permits use, sharing, adaptation, distribution and reproduction in any medium or format, as long as you give appropriate credit to the original author(s) and the source, provide a link to the Creative Commons license and indicate if changes were made.

The images or other third party material in this chapter are included in the chapter's Creative Commons license, unless indicated otherwise in a credit line to the material. If material is not included in the chapter's Creative Commons license and your intended use is not permitted by statutory regulation or exceeds the permitted use, you will need to obtain permission directly from the copyright holder.

The manufacturer's authorised representative in the EU is Springer Nature Customer Service Centre GmbH, Europaplatz 3, 69115 Heidelberg, Germany. If you have any concerns regarding our products, please contact ProductSafety@springernature.com

Printed and bound by CPI Group (UK) Ltd, Croydon, CR0 4YY

25/03/2026

02078223-0003